BRITAIN
IN OLD PHOTOGRAPHS

School days around
Tinker's Farm

Norman Bartlam

Sutton Publishing Limited
Phoenix Mill · Thrupp · Stroud
Gloucestershire · GL5 2BU

First published 2003

Copyright © Norman Bartlam, 2003

Title page photograph: Trescott Nursery, 1949.

British Library Cataloguing in Publication Data
A catalogue record for this book is available from the
British Library.

ISBN 0-7509-3149-3

Typeset in 10.5/13.5 Photina.
Typesetting and origination by
Sutton Publishing Limited.
Printed and bound in England by
J.H. Haynes & Co. Ltd, Sparkford.

A postcard of Barnsdale Crescent, 1958.

CONTENTS

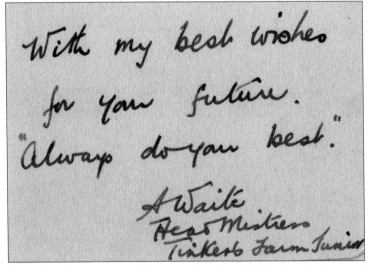

A good luck message written by Miss Amy Waite, headmistress of Tinker's Farm Junior School.

Wartime May Queen Betty Edwards.

Introduction

Any one walking in the countryside at the outer edge of Northfield in any of the years up to the 1920s would have been forgiven for thinking they were in the heart of the countryside. I suppose they really were! If you stopped any of the lads you had seen scrumping in the orchard, and told them that it was soon to be chopped down they would have thought you were an apple short of a full barrel! Imagine their shock when they found out a school was to be built there! If they had dashed across the fields to their homes and spoken to their parents they would have been told of rumours about houses being built. Soon enough the developers arrived and upset the applecart. The area was soon to be changed forever.

Man and machine devoured the countryside and before long the green and pleasant land was covered with over 2,000 houses. The growth continued across the city and Neville Chamberlain opened the 40,000th new house in 1933 at nearby Weoley Castle.

There was so much land that the council could afford to lay out the estates with semi-detached and small terraced houses, with more space between them than the traditional terraces of the inner city. Most had front and back gardens and were often laid out in a crescent formation with tree-lined pavements. This must have seemed amazing to those people who moved there from Ladywood. And there was still plenty of countryside around in which to play, although the number of orchards was decreasing.

At first the estates lacked the community facilities that existed in inner-city suburbs. It was realised that an estate was more than bricks and mortar. Shopping parades and community halls were set up which were run by local people. Allen's Cross was one of the first to have a community hall and it is still going strong after nearly seventy years of service.

The growth of the area led to a need for schools and demand outstripped supply. Both Trescott and Tinker's Farm Schools opened in temporary huts. Tinker's Farm Senior Mixed Council School, under the astute guidance of Miss Hilda Walmesley, was opened in 1931, and she later took on the headship of the secondary girls' school after the building was divided into two single-sex schools in 1933. Buildings for junior and infant pupils were opened on the site.

As the growth of the area continued it was deemed necessary to open two new primary schools with country sounding names: Ley Hill County Primary School opened in 1954 and Bellfield County Primary School in 1957. Sadly, by this time there were no fields left in which to grow apples for the teachers.

In 1967 the headteachers at the secondary schools, Miss Aslin and Mr Butler, both retired and the authority took the opportunity to draw up plans to merge the two single-sex schools into one new mixed school. The new school, Northfield Comprehensive School, opened in the former Tinker's Farm buildings in 1969 and became Northfield School in 1974.

In 1983 Northfield School celebrated the fiftieth anniversary of the building, becoming two single-sex schools, with an exhibition which attracted hundreds of visitors. The school continued to serve the small catchment area that it was built for successfully and modestly, until city council reorganisation in 1986. Northfield School became a victim of a changing policy that lead to the loss of small purpose-built community schools, in favour of what are said to be more economic schools.

At least the primary schools continue; Ley Hill and Bellfield are heading towards their fiftieth years and Trescott continues as the grand old man, having recently celebrated its seventieth anniversary.

I hope that you will find this book shows off the best of the schools from the past seventy years. Miss Aslin kept a particularly good photographic record of her school in the 1950s and Trescott has a good record from similar years. These photographs, together my own collection from the later years of Northfield School, form the basis of the book

I taught at Northfield School from 1980 until the school was closed by the local education authority in 1986. While there I researched the history of the schools and organised the fiftieth anniversary celebrations. A small booklet was produced and a special issue of the school newspaper Gallery was issued. While researching this book I have been astonished to find that so many people have kept these publications and treasure them. Naturally, I hope for a similar response to this book, as the schools have obviously played an enormous part in the community and have a place in the hearts of many thousands of people.

In 1953 The Tinker's Farm Chronicle school newspaper at Tinker's Farm Boys' School stated 'I hope you will keep the Chronicle as a memory of your school days and refer to it many times in the years to come'. The same comment applies to this book!

For many pupils Tinker's Farm has always been the apple of one's eye!

Norman Bartlam
January 2003

HEADTEACHERS

Tinker's Farm Senior Mixed Council School
    August 1931-February 1933   Miss H. Walmesley

Tinker's Farm Girls' School
    February 1933-December 1949   Miss H. Walmesley
    January 1950-July1967   Miss Aslin
    September 1967-July1969   Mrs B. Kendall (acting)

Tinker's Farm Boys' School
    February 1933-November 1933   Mr S. Blakey
    November 1933-July 1954   Mr T. Wright
    September 1954-July 1967   Mr F. Butler
    September 1967-July 1969   Mr D. Purser (acting)

Northfield Comprehensive School 1969-1974 and Northfield School 1974-1986
    September 1969-July 1979   Mr L. Green
    September 1979-December 1979   Mr C.J. Light (acting)
    January 1980-July 1986 Mr M. Evanson,   Mr C. James, Mrs Schnieder (acting)

1
The Early Years

Ley Hill Farmhouse, early 1920s.

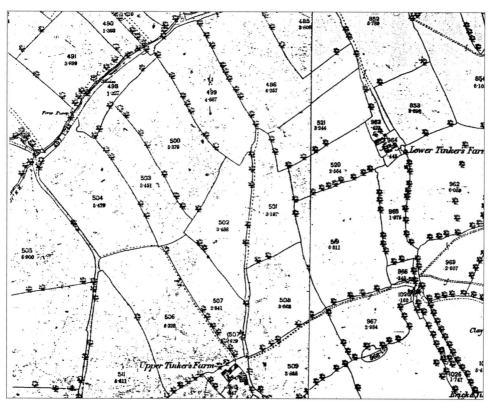

This map dates from 1884. It shows the rural nature of the area, with trees and field boundaries in abundance. The two farms were Upper Tinker's Farm and Lower Tinker's Farm. The name probably refers to tinkers who lived there, and not to a man called Tinker Fox. The tinkers were well known for mending kettles, pans and manufacturing horseshoes and nails. An 1851 survey indicates that the occupiers of the farms were Jonah Whitehouse and John Hollies.

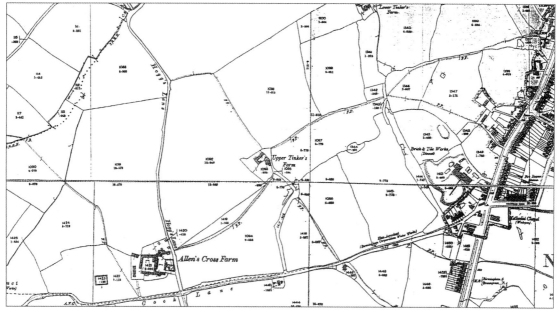

This more detailed map shows Upper Tinker's Farm and to the south-west, Allen's Cross Farm. The name Allen's Cross is thought to derive from a monk called Allen who put his preaching cross on the ground in AD 670 on the site where the present St Bartholomew's Church stands. Hogg's Lane was already named and Cock Lane became Frankley Beeches Road. St. Bartholomew's Church now occupies the site of Allen's Cross Farm. The Tinker's Farm schools were built on the site of Upper Tinker's Farm; more specifically, the site of the farmhouse was in the north-west of the school playground. The farm was likely to have been a mixed arable and pasture farm, owned in the 1840s by the Revd William Holden but run by tenant farmer John Hollies. The often talked about, but rarely seen, Tinker's Farm ghost was, apparently, a farmhand who disappeared one day. Many years later his remains were found at the bottom of the well.

This section of map shows the Ley Hill area in 1884. The large wooded area is Cutler's Rough; the housing estate built off Bell Holloway in recent years has a street named after the wood. To the south-east of it lies Hogg's Farm which it has been suggested is named after a Mr Hogg, hence also Hogg's Lane. Ley Hill Farm can clearly be seen, as can the lane which ran along the eastern side of the map which was to become the Holloway. At the top of it is Ley Hill House, which was the home of the chocolate and cake manufacturer Christian Kunzle, who ran Scotland Farm, which is also seen on the map.

Ley Hill House when it was in the in the hands of the City Council, April 2000. Shamefully it was allowed to fall into disrepair, and in spite of protests it was demolished in May 2002.

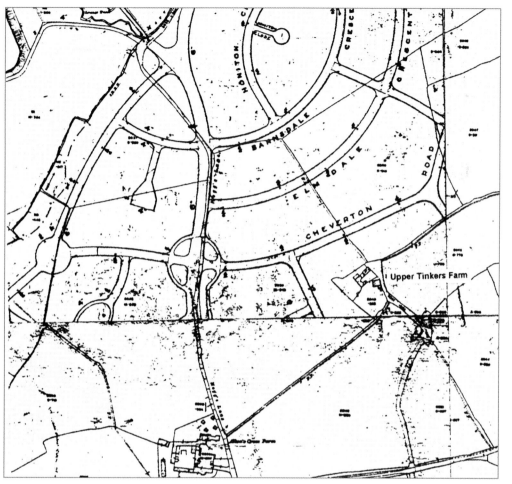

This map was drawn up in 1916 and shows the basic outline for some of the roads to be built on what was to become the Allen's Cross/Tinker's Farm estate. Notice how Hogg's Lane was widened, but kept to its original line for most of its length. The crescent-shaped roads were given rural names such as Elmdale and Barnsdale.

The first Tinker's Farm Girl's School badge contained a tinker's cauldron, symbolising the metal manufacturers, and a sheaf of corn to represent the agricultural heritage of the area. The first Headmistress of the school, Miss H.R. Walmesley, once spoke about a walk from Selly Oak to the Lickey Hills. She came across some men cutting down an apple orchard, and they told her that a school was to be built. 'Little did I think', she said, 'that it was the school to which I should come.' Later, at the time of the school's twenty-first anniversary celebrations she told the local press: 'In the orchard there was a pond, surrounded by a bank of mud on which water wagtails were disporting themselves as they had done for centuries, and the water wagtails still returned every year though the pond had been filled in and built over. When the school opened it consisted of four huts and at the first assembly 300 boys and girls, drawn from ten different schools, stood on a cinder track – to avoid the mud – and under no roof but the sky.' Long before the orchard was cut down plans were being made to build a housing estate on the land to house Birmingham's expanding population.

The estate at Allen's Cross was one of a number of planned estates that were built in the late 1920s and early 1930s. The *Birmingham Post* on 27 May 1929 reported that the school, which was to become Tinker's Farm, was to be built to accommodate 432 infants and juniors and 800 senior children 'at a cost of £41,300'. On 31 January 1930 the City of Birmingham Education Committee was told that 'the first pair of temporary classrooms are now in the course of erection'. The buildings were 'placed on the site so as to permit another department being erected should the need arise at some future date'.

This aerial photograph shows the area that roughly corresponds with the above map. The Tinker's Farm schools can be seen in the middle top. The large traffic island on the right is the junction of Hogg's Lane and Cheverton Road.

> 24.8.31.   This school was opened in the hutments Tinkers Farm, on Monday August 24th 1931. 327 children were entered, the majority of were transferred from the following schools:-
>
>   Stirchley Street,   Senior Boys.
>   Cotteridge,   Senior Girls.
>   Kings Norton,   Mixed.
>   Trescott Rd.   Junior.
>   Tinkers Farm   Junior.
>   North field   C. of E.
>
> Eight members of Staff and a Head Teacher were appointed; eight classes were formed.
> For staff list see reference page.

> 2. 2. 33 School finished at afternoon session preparatory to division into separate departments.

An extract from the Tinker's Farm logbook for 24 August 1931 (top). Trescott Road School opened earlier, under the direction of Mr John Blundell, on 8 June 1931. It is recorded that most of the 371 children 'came to school in their shoes covered in clay and ashes, as the school had been built on made up ground'. The Tinker's Farm building opened in the temporary huts on 24 August 1931. There were nine staff and 327 children, both boys and girls, but in February 1933 (above) 'School finished at afternoon session preparatory to division into separate departments', and the school was re-organised into separate single sex schools. The boys went downstairs and the girls upstairs, and it stayed like that until 1969. It is recorded that on its first day there were 336 boys on the roll with ages ranging from ten to fourteen years. The 336 were made up of 298 boys transferring from the mixed school, 23 from Trescott Juniors and 15 from Tinkers Farm Road Juniors.

As the local population continued to grow, the need for more accommodation became necessary. The *Birmingham Gazette* reported in June 1935 that 'Plans have been prepared for the erection of a department for infants at Tinker's Farm. This step is rendered necessary by the pressure on the existing accommodation. The building will include six classrooms and a large room for the youngest children.' It was estimated that the building would cost £9,400. From 1 January 1936, during building work, temporary accommodation was provided in the Northfield Methodist Church Sunday School room. Later in the year, on 24 August, further temporary accommodation was obtained at the Allen's Cross Community Hall, which was rented for £5 a week. The infant block was completed in 1937. Then the Tinker's Farm infants were transferred to the new infant block and the other building became juniors only. In later years the infant block became the secondary school's Upper School, and when the junior school moved out their building became the expanded secondary school's craft block.

This is the wedding of the oldest son of the caretaker at Tinker's Farm in the early 1940s. Of additional interest is the hut on the left, which is the original school building mentioned in the extract opposite. Notice also the open veranda-type walls on the main building to the right.

Betty Taylor, the daughter of the caretaker at Tinker's Farm, stands outside their house at 41 Tinker's Farm Road, 1933. Mr Taylor not only had the cleaning to do but also had to stoke the boiler and attend to evening classes, as well as activities such as the Boys' Brigade and Bible classes. Mrs Taylor had the job of doing the laundry for the school: sixty or more roller towels, dusters and table clothes were all boiled up on the standard cast-iron gas cooker with four burners, on which all the school meals were cooked. In the house there was only one electric power plug which had a 4-inch square iron case, and a glowing orange light when switched on: it was used for the wireless and to plug the iron in to press all the school washing, which was dried on the school radiators after the school was closed and collected at about 7.00 a.m.

The first photograph of the staff at Tinker's Farm Senior Mixed School. *Back row, left to right*: Mr Collins, Miss Chesterton, Miss Sheppard, Mr Leonard, Miss Hill, Mr Fulwood, Miss Gill, Mr Baines. *Front row*: Miss Baker, Miss Harrison, Miss Blackmore, Miss Walmesley the headmistress, Mr Matthews, Miss Dalton, Miss Ede. Miss Walmesley was the foundation headmistress at Tinker's Farm and took over the Girls' School when the school was split into single sex schools in February 1933. Mr Blakey was appointed headmaster of the Boys' School and Thomas Wright took over from him later that year, when Mr Blakey left to take over as Superintendent of the Shenley Field Cottage Homes. Miss Walmesley remained until 1949 and Mr Wright until 1954.

Miss Walmesley was well thought of in school, in the local area and in education circles. An inspector's report in 1936 called attention to her 'cheerfulness, courage and intelligence in facing the many difficulties of organization arising from fluctuations in numbers and age range and from changes in staff. Her thoughtful planning of schemes and systematic review of work have been a great value to the staff.' The report added: 'the school has become a real force in the neighbourhood. The influence of the Headmistress is not confined to the girls: it extends to the flourishing Old Scholars' Association and to the parents who are kept in close touch with the work and play of the school.'

Left: The first known photograph of the staff at Tinker's Farm Girls' School, 1933. Miss Walmesley is in the centre. She was awarded an honorary MA degree at Birmingham University in 1933 because of her role as president of the National Union of Women Teachers.

Headmaster Thomas Wright came to Tinker's Farm from Elkington School and quickly established himself in his new role. A report by the school inspectorate in 1937 concluded: 'the headmaster has not only shown a sound conception of his interesting task but has also fully realized his opportunity for providing his boys with a curriculum which satisfies their several interests and at the same time meets their varied needs, and he and his staff are to be congratulated on the healthy corporate life which has been established.' He is pictured with Mr Ingley and Mr Blackmore during a school trip to London in about 1950. Mr Wright retired in 1954 after nearly twenty-one years at the school.

Right: Dorothy Morton, née Gardener, one of the foundation pupils at Tinker's Farm, with a blouse she made in a hobbies lesson. She is seen at a display which incorporates her work at Northfield School's fiftieth anniversary celebrations.

A group of former pupils from Tinker's Farm who were at the school in 1931. They are pictured here in the main hall at Northfield School during the fiftieth anniversary celebrations.

Cock Lane, now Frankley Beeches Road, 1934.

Pupils from Tinker's Farm are put through their paces during a PE lesson, 1935. One of the girls is Madge Moore. The buildings behind are in Kelby Close.

The same view in 1983.

This photograph from the Trescott Infant School album is a colour print dating from the late 1930s or early 1940s, which means it is fairly rare. The typed caption states: 'there are a great many country walks and outings which the children of this school may take – and natural specimens etc are always at hand. In the springtime the school is very naturally decorated with bluebells gathered on nature walks and at weekends.'

The rural nature of the area is clearly seen in this view of workers at Hogg's Farm, *c*. 1910. The farm, like others in the area, was established at the time of the first field enclosures in about 1583. Today the farm lies below Frankley Reservoir.

An aerial view of the Frankley and Bartley Green waterworks and reservoir at the Northfield end of the Elan Valley Aqueduct, 1949. King Edward VII, accompanied by Queen Alexandra, officially opened the waterworks at the Elan Valley in July 1904. Parliamentary powers were obtained in 1922 to acquire land at Bartley Green for the purpose of a new reservoir in a valley adjoining the Frankley Works. A contract for the 500 million-gallon reservoir was placed in 1925 and the new reservoir was inaugurated on 19 July 1930.

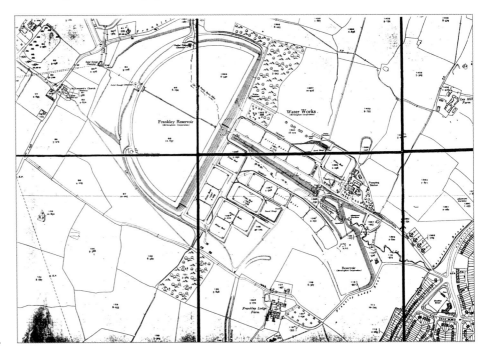

Frankley Reservoir was built on land once occupied by Hogg's Farm. This 1937 map shows the two nearest farms that survived the soaking, namely Frankley Lodge Farm to the south of the map and Ley Hill Farm in the north-east. St Leonard's Church remained in the north-west.

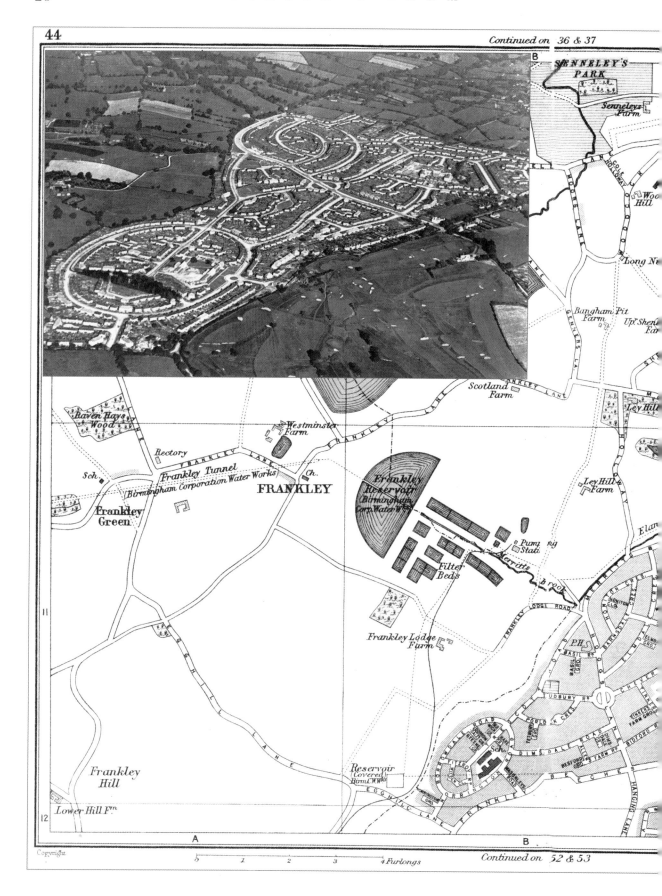

Continued on 36 & 37

44

SENNELEY'S PARK

Senneleys Farm

Woo Hill

Long Ne

Bangham Pit Farm

Up Shen Far

Scotland Farm

Ley Hill

Raven Hays Wood

Westminster Farm

Rectory

Frankley Tunnel

Sch.

Birmingham Corporation Water Works

Ch.

FRANKLEY

Frankley Reservoir
Birmingham Corp. Water W'ks

Ley Hill Farm

Frankley Green

Pumping Stati

Filter Beds

Merritts

brook

Frankley Lodge Road

P.H.

Frankley Lodge Farm

Frankley Hill

Reservoir (Covered) Birm C.W.W.

Lower Hill F'm.

11

12

A

B

Continued on 52 & 53

0   1   2   3   4 Furlongs

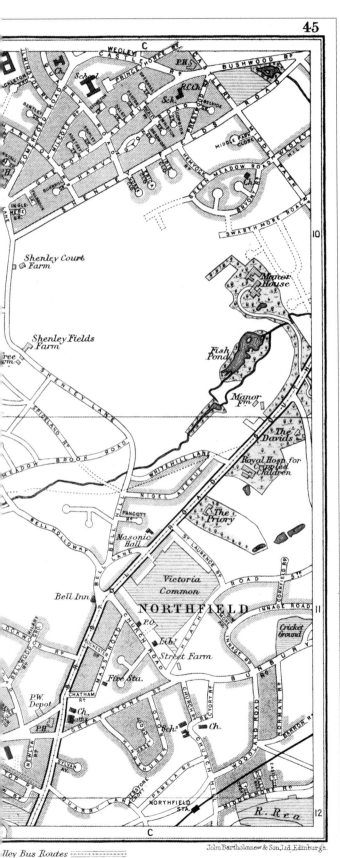

There was some criticism of estates such as Allen's Cross in that they consisted mainly of housing, so attempts were made to introduce community buildings. The Allen's Cross Community Centre on Tinker's Farm is the oldest purpose-built community centre in the city. It was opened in 1932 by George Cadbury and quickly became the focal point of community activities.

A magazine was established to keep people informed about what was happening: it was produced with neighbouring estates under the title *The Weoley Castle & Allen's Cross Review*. The January 1935 edition featured the 'Giant Bazaar' which was held to raise funds for 'the erection of a Club House at the rear of the Hall'.

Mr Cadbury was guest of honour at the bazaar and he noted that similar halls were opening across the city. 'At last the City Council have realised that such halls were necessary to the estates', he said, adding 'the work is not done by officials, but by the people – the people who live on the estates'. The hall had been 'a veritable godsend to the estate'. The magazine mentioned the sewing class, which was preparing for a visit to Bird's Custard Powder factory; the Co-operative Guild, which was looking at peace and education; the Sunday Morning adult school; and the table tennis coaching scheme. The magazine also included a section called 'Hints for the Housewife', which stated: 'Newspaper is useful for cleaning windows, polishing the cooking range, and, if applied immediately after cooking, for removing the grease from the stove.'

Inset: The estates, mid- to late 1930s. The Allen's Cross estate was one of the largest estates built in the interwar period, although only half the size of Kingstanding, it had 2,161 dwellings, all of which were built in geometric patterns. This road pattern was criticised by some as being monotonous, although houses were built in blocks of two, four or six, and had much better façades than traditional inner-city housing.

Relaxation for the workers was provided when The Beeches pub was built at the corner of Hogg's Lane and Barnsdale Crescent.

The best-known pub was, and still is, the Black Horse on Bristol Road. Don't be fooled by the mock-Tudor design, for it is not as old as it looks. It is pictured here under construction in 1928. It was the third pub to be built on the site.

Just off the estates are the swimming baths, built on Bristol Road and opened on 8 May 1937 to provide facilities for the whole of Northfield. The population had in the main moved from inner-city areas where homes rarely had indoor baths. The new Northfield homes were built with bathrooms, so it was deemed not necessary for washing baths to be provided at the swimming baths. In 1946 it was recorded that only 537 out of 13,000 houses were without a bathroom in Northfield, whereas 5,165 of 6,500 homes in Ladywood did not have a bathroom! Today the pool has over 440,000 visitors per year and is undergoing a multi-million pound refurbishment.

The leisure facilities at Northfield pool extended to this state-of-the-art café. Customers could relax and talk over the news of the day, and indeed much was happening in the world. Two days before the centre opened the giant airship *Hindenburg* exploded in a ball of fire and four days after the opening saw the Coronation of King George VI and Queen Elizabeth.

St Bartholomew's Church was built on the highest point of Hoggs Lane near the Frankley Beeches Road junction in 1937.

Lily Maynard was the May Queen at Tinker's Farm Girls' School in 1937. When interviewed for Northfield School's fiftieth anniversary celebrations she said: 'As the May Queen I chose my own flowers for a crown. I chose Lily of the Valley. I felt it was the most exciting thing that had ever happened to me. At the end of the ceremony we had the "revels" – each class performed a little play. The whole school was involved, and there was a great feeling of festivity.' The hall was lavishly decorated with flowers, mainly bluebells and white may. Miss Chesterton was usually in charge of the decorations.

The Allen's Cross and Tinker's Farm estates grew so rapidly that it proved necessary to build an infants' school on the Tinker's Farm site, and when it opened on 5 April 1937 the building had not even been completed! In that week the government unveiled a new 'green belt' policy, initially to contain suburban sprawl around London, but for the Tinker's Farm Infants' School headmistress, Florence Farrow, and her teaching staff of Miss Whele, Miss Walker, Miss Kerkin, Miss Milroy, Miss Whitall, Miss Ballard and Mrs Whetnall there were more mundane things to be sorted out. The logbook later mentions a visit by the school inspector who made 'suggestions concerning lavatories, towel rails and shelves for dental purposes'.

> I, Florence Glendy Farrow, opened this School as a separate Infants' Department on April 5th 1937.
>
> The number of Infants and Juniors, together, having risen to seventeen classes, it became necessary to open the Infants' Department before building operations were complete.
>
> The Hall, the Reception Class Room two cloakrooms, the Girls' Lavatories and much of the playground cannot yet be used.
>
> The Reception Class is being held in the Medical Room.
>
> The number on Roll on the opening day was 290.

Offence	Amount of Punishment
Jumping through hedge in school	1 stroke each hand
lawn	1 " "
	1 -
Repeated inattention	1 stroke
Ungentlemanly conduct in play ground	1 stroke in each hand
Deliberate maltreatment of tools	4 strokes.
Spelling mistake	1 stroke on hand
Disregard of Cloapin Corris	1 - -
Repeated inattention	1 - -
Talking at the wrong time - inattention	1 " " "
	1 " "
Rough conduct in Classroom during play	1 " -
Careless work	1 - - -
Wasting time	1 - -

An extract from the punishment book at Tinker's Farm Boys' School, 1937. Smoking in school and shooting paper pellets also incurred the penalty of one stroke on the hand!

The May Festival was a yearly event at Tinker's Farm Girls' School between 1935 and 1959. The festival centred on the investiture of a May Queen, who was elected by pupils. The May Queen was in her final year, became head girl and crowned the following May Queen.

The runner up in the voting became the Herald. The first May Queen in 1935 was Beryl Cheshire. The other May Queens in this decade were Rose Ford (1936), Lillian Maynard (1937), Beatrice Holyoak (1938), and Alma Brooks (1939).

The Coronation ceremony took place in front of the whole school. The retiring May Queen gave a farewell speech, and then the abdication ceremony took place. The Herald announced the name of her successor and the singing of 'Come Lovely Queen' took place. The procession re-entered for the crowning ceremony and everyone sang the 'The May Queen's Song'. After the crowning ceremony each class performed a little a play under the collective name of 'the revels'.

Alma Brooks (left) and Betty Edwards, the May Queens of 1939 and 1940, pictured above at the front, met at an event held at Northfield Library in July 2000. Behind with the cap is Martin Berry who taught at the school in the 1980s and ran the highly successful school band, The Alibis.

The international language Esperanto, a common tongue for world use, was taught at Tinker's Farm Girls' School, and the school became well known across Europe such was the enthusiasm for the language, which was promoted by Miss Walmesley. Esperanto was devised by a Dr Zamenhof in Poland and it is based on the simplification of numerous languages. Its grammar consists of only sixteen rules with no exceptions, while the key words have been selected mainly from the most widely known words in European languages. It was said to be easy to learn and easy to speak – a way of communicating across national barriers and of gaining a wider view of the world. The idea began at Tinker's Farm because Miss Walmesley was keen on languages, was a member of the League of Nations and travelled widely. She and Miss Waite of Tinker's Farm Primary School introduced Esperanto to the curriculum to help to foster peaceful understanding. It started in the secondary school as a twenty-minute club run in the lunch period by Miss Sheppard. Doris Satchwell, a pupil at the school in the 1930s, went on to become Baroness Fisher of Rednal and was President of the Parliamentarian Esperantists. During the Easter holidays in 1937 an International Esperanto School was held at Tinker's Farm with twenty visiting girls, mainly from France. The *Birmingham Post* reported: 'This is probably the first camp of its kind that has ever been held and the Tinkers Farm Senior Girls' School is one of the very few schools in this country in which Esperanto has a place on the curriculum.' The following year forty girls, accompanied by Miss Walmesley, Miss Sheppard, Miss Atkins and Miss Sawyer, attended a congress in Holland. There was a leaving party for Miss Sheppard, who had to leave teaching because she was due to be married.

Esperanto was performed as one of the revels at the first May Festival in 1935. Beryl Cheshire was crowned the May Queen.

Esperantists from the early 1930s returned to the school building and met up again at Northfield School's fiftieth anniversary celebrations. The group includes Betty Heywood, Doreen Wheelwright, Violet Hodgetts, Dorothy Kilgour, Bridget Aitken, née Dennelly, and Enid Lloyd.

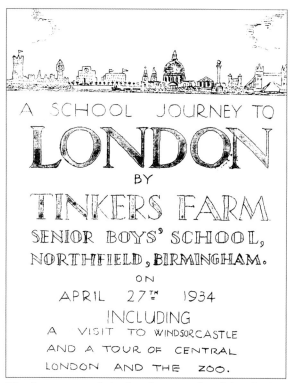

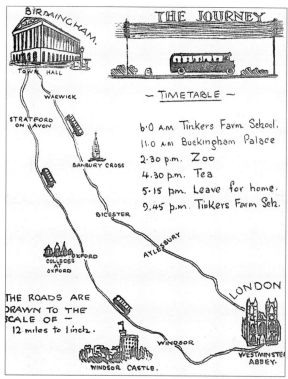

The front cover of the brochure produced for the first school journey by pupils of Tinker's Farm Senior Boys' School, 1934. Ten teachers took a party of 192 children on a sightseeing trip around the capital. In the days before fast coaches and motorways the journey to Buckingham Palace took five hours: the coaches left school at 6.00 a.m. The school logbook records: 'a great deal of credit is due to Mr Leonard and especially to Mr Collins for the excellent descriptive and illustrated booklet they drew up'.

In 1937 the fourth annual journey of Tinker's Farm Senior Boys' School was to Liverpool, where 250 pupils and teachers visited the Mersey Tunnel, Overhead Railway, and the liner *Abosso*, then took a ferry to New Brighton. The brochure included a sketch of the tunnel compared with the distance from Northfield to Selly Oak and a scale drawing of the liner compared to the size of the school. At the time of Northfield School's fiftieth anniversary celebrations Ronald Pickering

wrote: 'I remember with a great deal of joy the day trips that the school took us on. The one to London was a big day out and possibly even to this day the most exciting thing that was ever undertaken by a naïve and wet behind the ears child of eleven years. The cost was a staggering 10s, and we had to save for the trip at 1s per week. Do bear in mind that at this time Northfield was a farming village and bears no resemblance to the busy conurbation that it is today. These were great days for me and my schoolmates of the day.'

2

The War Years

Tinker's Farm pupils Dig for Victory!

> 83 1939
> Mon. Sept. 4th   As England declared war on Germany yesterday the school is closed until further notice.

Miss Walmesley wrote in her school's logbook: 'War is declared. The work of education comes to a standstill.' Mr Wright wrote: 'As England declared war on Germany yesterday the school is closed until further notice.' At the outbreak of war the schools were closed, but parents' meetings were arranged and homework given before the schools reopened in October 1939, although compulsory education didn't return until January 1940. Contracts were awarded for the erection of nine shelters on the Tinker's Farm site at a cost of £1,085! Infant pupils at Tinker's Farm were said to have accepted an ARP practice 'as an enjoyable experience, being curious to see inside the shelters, and not at all nervous'. Plans were drawn up for pupils who lived within five minutes' walk of the school to go home in the event of an air raid warning. Many children were evacuated to South Wales, mainly to Bedlinog, Bargoed, Gelligaer, Ystrad Mynach and Trelewis, near Newport. An entry in the Tinker's Farm Boys' School logbook in July 1942 reads: 'This afternoon all but a few boys brought their respirators to school and wore them for ten minutes. A small number of the respirators were found to be faulty or too small and the owners were directed to their warden and/or the ARP depot at the Grange Bristol Road South.'

What better way could the girls at Tinkers Farm show that they were working as near to normal as possible than to continue with the May Festival? So, in May 1940 Betty Edwards became the first wartime and the sixth May Queen. The school logbook records 'a full repertory of plays and dances given, very successful and pleasant'. The school closed the following day for Whitsuntide, but was reassembled 'by government order' on 14 May: 'about 75 per cent of children were present.' The infants' school logbook records that a Christmas party was held in December 1941 preceded by a performance of *Sleeping Beauty*, 'the staff cheerfully groped around in the school in the blackout in order to clear up after all the events of an exceptionally busy Christmastide'.

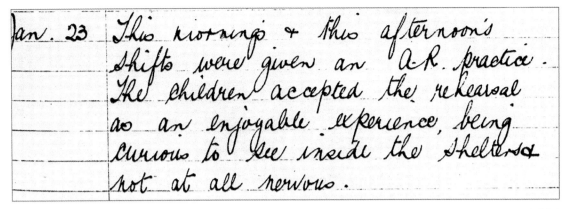

Jan. 23 This morning & this afternoon's shifts were given an A.R. practice. The children accepted the rehearsal as an enjoyable experience, being curious to see inside the shelters & not at all nervous.

5th Sept. 1940 Air Raid last night & this am. Air Raid this morning during assembly. Plane heard, guns fired etc. All children were in the shelters in a very short time. Raider Passed was sounded in about 15 minutes.

Nov. 13 Air Raid Warning 12.45 — 2.30.pm. Air Raid warning 3.55 — 5.5. Bombs dropped in neighbourhood. Cannon, anti aircraft & machine gun fire.

Tinker's Farm lay outside the 'government danger zone' for evacuation purposes, but as these logbook entries record the area came under attack during the heavy raids of August 1940. The 'severe air raid' of 26 August 1940 was the one that destroyed the Market Hall in the Bull Ring. The logbook entry of 5 September 1940 reads: 'Air raid this morning during assembly. Plane heard, guns fired, etc. All children were in the shelters in a very short time. Lasted for 15 minutes.' Mrs Bennett recalls being in a friend's house on Tinker's Farm Road when a 'plane seemed to circle over the school, perhaps looking for the Austin [factory]. It dived on top of us – we dived under the table. Through the windows we could see it coming towards us. He turned spiteful and peppered the dustbins; we could hear it peppering them up the road. It eventually flew off and as we looked out of the back window we saw two black things fall from it – these were two bombs, which landed near the Austin. I think one of them killed a man on the railway track.' When Northfield School produced the magazine *Tinker's Farm at War* William Coombs-Lewis wrote to recall an evening raid over the city. 'I came out of Northfield picture house; the whole of the village was lit up. We thought the whole place was on fire, but it was the glow from the city centre.' Olive Coombs-Lewis remembers that 'a land mine once dropped near Quinney's Farm and a shell dropped in Dimsdale Grove. We heard it whistling as it came down. Mother slammed the door and pushed us to the ground!' During November 1940 the boys' school logbook records: 'Bombs dropped in neighbourhood. Cannon, anti-aircraft and machine-gun fire.' Six people were killed and twenty-five injured at the Longbridge car factory, which had come under the direction of the Ministry of Aircraft Production (the wings and fuselage of nearly 3,000 aircraft were made there during the war). This was the month when Coventry was decimated. In Birmingham steps were made for evacuation of pupils in the outer areas, and accordingly in February 1941 over a hundred Tinker's Farm pupils went to Gelligaer and surrounding towns in South Wales, so missing the heavy raids over the city in April 1941. The junior school secretary Mrs Edwards recalls: 'Many pupils returned within three weeks of being evacuated as they did not like being away from home in such unfamiliar surroundings.'

The 'Dig for Victory' campaign was taken very seriously at Tinker's Farm. The gardens between the school buildings were given over to the growing of crops of fruit and vegetables. A sentence in a 1945 logbook refers to the 'good crop of potatoes'. Up to eighty boys, often under the direction of Mr Ingley, helped farmers on Lower Shenley, Upper Shenley, Lower Hill and Yew Tree Farms with potato picking. At certain times prisoners of war also helped in the fields, a big purple patch on their uniforms identifying them, though they were never in contact with the pupils. The 1940 harvest festival at the infants' school had a 'good response from staff and children' and 'fruit, vegetables and groceries were sent to hospitals etc'. Mr Wright was chairman of a committee that was responsible for a stall in the Market Hall in the Bull Ring during the food production campaigns. In September 1942 two boys, Fred Morris and John Porter, went to the Council House to receive 15s Saving Certificates, prizes for essays about the Food Exhibition.

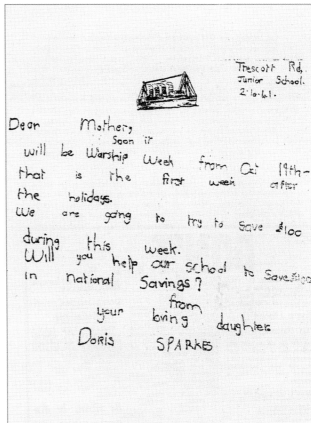

Above, left: Tinker's Farm at War was a highly successful booklet produced by Northfield School. As the title suggests, it gave an account of the schools during the period 1939–45. It contains numerous extracts from the school logbooks and accounts of people who were there at the time. Mr Wright at the boys' school kept a particularly detailed account of the war and how it affected his school. *Above, right:* Warship Week was a morale-boosting fund-raising campaign held in 1941 to raise money for the war effort. A pupil at Trescott School wrote this letter. Tinker's Farm Boys' School raised a staggering £256 3s 6d. Other fund-raising activities included knitting balaclavas, gloves and scarves for the forces. Occasionally pupils made blouses and coats out of sheets and blankets, and underwear from parachute silk.

Peter Mallinder was a 14-year-old pupil at Tinker's Farm when he drew this pen and ink sketch in 1945. He says it 'shows the view from Mr Wright's office and clearly shows the balcony. The classroom in the centre downstairs was Mr Froggatt's class 3A or 2A at the time. The bicycle belonged to Mr Greenaway or Mr Froggatt'.

	Morning	Afternoon
Monday	1 ton **15** cwt	1 ton **5** cwt
Tuesday	**2** tons	1 ton **10** cwt.
Wednesday	1 ton **5** cwt.	1 ton
Thursday	1 ton **15** cwt.	**15** cwt.
Friday	**2** tons **5** cwt.	**2** tons
Saturday	**3** tons	**2** tons **5** cwt.

Set 70.

How much coal did he sell all day on :—

1. Wednesday 2. Tuesday 3. Friday 4. Saturday
5. Monday

How many bags of coal did he sell on :—

6. Wednesday afternoon 7. Friday afternoon
8. Saturday morning 9. Monday afternoon
10. Thursday morning

Set 71.

On which afternoons did he sell :—

1. **20** cwt. 2. **40** cwt. 3. **30** cwt. 4. **25** cwt.?
5. **45** cwt.?

Which was :—.

6. His best morning 7. His best afternoon 8. His
best day 9. His worst morning 10. His worst day

Trescott Infant School, 1941. A note in the school's album reads: 'In 1941 a radiogram was bought and wireless lessons were taken by various classes in the Infant School.' This is a photograph of a group of six-year-old children taking part in Ann Driver's rhythmic lesson. The note adds: 'Many classes, by means of the loudspeaker extension, have enjoyed and taken part in the stories and dramatisation. This radiogram has been of invaluable use in the Nursery. A large collection of records has been bought for this purpose including Derek McCulloch's animal noises, hymns, and Nursery Rhymes.' In December 1941 the staff at Trescott Infant School decided to form a rota in order to look after the young children of war workers. The children paid 1½d per day and were given a bottle of milk and 1d-worth of biscuits. A play centre was opened in January 1942 for which each child paid 7½d per week.

Extracts from a mathematics book in use at Tinker's Farm Junior School in 1943.

Iris Pemberton, who was crowned May Queen on 20 May 1942 parades in the playground before junior pupils. Miss Walmesley wrote in the log book: 'A very happy day.' The festival was repeated for old girls and up to 500 attended. Sheila Thompson recalls: 'the May Festivals were all very democratically handled. Pupils from the top classes would nominate whoever they thought was suitable, taking into account their achievements, standard of work and behaviour of the said girl. There would also be Maids of Honour, chosen from the twelve other classes. Everything was a hive of activity preceding the event. Mothers went frantically trying to cadge extra clothing coupons from relatives. Dads' "Dig for Victory" pots were raided to find suitable flowers for the long-handled baskets carried by the attendants. One of the big solid high chairs used by teachers in the class would be used for the throne, bedecked with purple velvet. And suddenly the day arrived. The assembly hall was hushed and the ceremony began. All was performed in complete silence, except for the music of Mendelssohn and the rustling of pristine white taffeta.'

> 19.7.44 Open day for parents. The school was open for visits of parents. A large number came – about 200. They were thoughtful interested and very observant and appreciative. It was very satisfactory to experience the live interest which they had – both fathers and mothers in their childrens education, especially since this interest has withstood the strain of five war years.

Parental involvement in the children's work was actively encouraged and staff were pleased with the response to events such as open days and parents' evenings. Excitement mounted at the beginning of May 1945 as VE Day neared. The Tinker's Farm Girls' logbook records: 'School closed – cessation of war in Europe after 5 years and 9 months.'

Betty Gayler was crowned May Queen in 1943. Other activities of the year included a talk from the Ministry of Information on life in Nigeria, the annual garden party for Esperantists, and 150 girls opened accounts in the Birmingham Municipal Bank. Parents' Day in July saw a very large attendance 'in spite of the many difficulties which limit their time for visit'. Miss Walmesley wrote in the log book: 'There was a remarkably friendly approach to the work, marked appreciation of the school, intelligent appraisement of their own child's progress, and a most pleasing interest generally on the educational side. Considering that this is the fourth year of the war, the response was as good as it was remarkable.'

The 1945 May Festival was held six days after the school reopened following the VE Day holiday. Pauline Timerick was crowned May Queen. Eight plays and a dance were performed. Two evening ceremonies 'produced a very happy audience of parents and girls'. At the end of term the school was renamed Tinker's Farm Secondary Modern School for Girls. The form teachers were Miss Hill, Miss Sawyer, Miss Freeman, Miss Chesterton, Miss Gilberthorpe, Miss Wood, Miss Vaughan and Miss Blackmore.

3
Postwar 1940s

The war is over so let's get down to work! Trescott Nursery, *c.* 1946.

Out for a stroll in the sunshine along Wilden Close, 1940s.

The same view, 2002.

The Trescott Infant School album notes: 'the school is modern. It was opened in 1931. It is a veranda type school. All the classrooms open on both sides with doors on to a large open asphalt playground. Here children enjoy free play with hoops.'

In March 1947 two Trescott pupils, Doreen Taylor and Christopher Westwood appeared on the cover of a booklet entitled *Learning to Live* which was a publication produced to commemorate the Birmingham Education Week.

'Free' activity at Trescott Infant School, 1947. The note in the school album reads: 'we decided that to follow on the Nursery routine the first hour of each morning should be devoted to activities. Material is provided for water and sand play, modelling with plasticine or clay, sewing or knitting, reading or writing. The staff and children collect waste material of all kinds. The girl on the bottom left is making animals out of plasticine and clay.'

Northfield's primary schools often played host to pupils from inner-city schools who visited their counterparts in their semi-rural settings. Many of the inner-city pupils may never have seen the countryside before, or indeed a view that was not obliterated by factories or houses. Did the Northfield pupils realise how lucky they were as they hosted their visitors? In 1948 100 pupils from Benson Road School in Winson Green visited Trescott and were taken to Frankley Beeches to admire the view. The local press reported on the school exchange and pictured the children on a nature walk, picking flowers and blackberries and generally enjoying themselves in the open fields. On another occasion forty-two children from Rea Street School in the heart of Digbeth visited Trescott and took in the tremendous view looking towards Frankley Beeches. The horse-drawn hay collector plods on in the distance.

Pupils picking flowers on a nature walk, 1948.

Another view of one of the late 1940s exchange visits with pupils from inner-city Birmingham. The press reported that 'they were seen walking through hay fields and enjoying the rough and tumble of the hay'.

Pupils from Benson Road School invited their semi-rural friends to see their inner-city environment. Pupils were given a tour of a local glass manufactory. Ten-year-old Maurice Burrows tried his hand at glass blowing. The local press stated: 'for most of the visitors a factory represented a new and exciting adventure. When they finally took their leave, they must have felt proud to make new friends who lived and worked in much the same way, but who were surrounded by shops and factories instead of hills and fields'.

In 1948 this letter was sent to Trescott Road School following a visit by pupils and staff from St. Peter's RC School, which was on Broad Street. That school has now been demolished and part of the International Convention Centre stands on its site. Everyone clearly enjoyed the visit to the countryside and the headmistress seemed to enjoy her blackberries! Following one visit the local press reported: ' how to be a good host does not normally form part of the school syllabus,' but these visits 'were by schools who want to know and understand boys and girls in other schools'.

CITY OF BIRMINGHAM EDUCATION COMMITTEE

St Peter's RC SCHOOL ...Mixed... DEPT. Oct.14. 1948.

Dear Miss Doyle.

Please accept my thanks with that of the children for the very happy afternoon that we spent with you on Thursday last. It was indeed a real treat for our city bairns to see such beautiful country, & I enjoyed it myself as much as they did.

With renewed gratitude for your hospitality & trouble

Yours very sincerely,

Marjorie Clements.

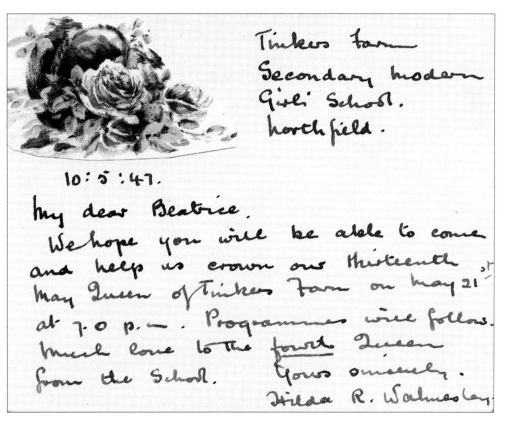

Tinkers Farm
Secondary Modern
Girls' School.
Northfield.

10:5:47.

My dear Beatrice.
    We hope you will be able to come
and help us crown our thirteenth
May Queen of Tinkers Farm on May 21st
at 7.0 p.m. Programmes will follow.
Much love to the fourth Queen
from the School.
                        Yours sincerely.
                        Hilda R. Walmesley.

A handwritten invitation from Miss Walmesley to Beatrice Holyoake, who was the fourth Tinker's Farm May Queen in 1938, inviting her to attend the investiture of the thirteenth May Queen, Marjorie Nash, in 1947. The other postwar May Queens in the 1940s were Pauline Timerick (1945), Brenda Bladon (1946), Patricia Lambert (1948) and Grace McGann (1949).

Along with many other children in the country we closed our school in honour of the wedding of H.R.H. Princess Margaret and Mr Anthony Armstrong. Most of our children had an exciting day watching it on television. Princess Margaret wore a long white flowing dress with a vale to match. When she went on her honeymoon she wore a yellow cost-um and a yellow hat.

HRH Princess Margaret on her wedding day in 1947, painted by a pupil from Trescott School. The accompanying text in the school album reads: 'Along with many other children in the country we closed our school in honour of the wedding of HRH Princess Margaret and Mr Anthony Armstrong. Most of the children had an exciting day watching it on television. Princess Margaret wore a long white dress with a veil to match. When she went on her honeymoon she wore a yellow costume and a yellow hat.'

Esperanto students with letters from their pen pals, 1946. Doris Tack is second left on the back row.

Extracts from an Esperanto book used at Tinker's Farm Junior School in the 1940s. The book was written by the school's headmistress Miss Waite and sold in the Midland Educational shop in Corporation Street.

Tinker's Farm Infant School, 1946. Josie Cardall née Moore says: 'I am on the right of the two girls who are holding hands on the back row. This was a spring pageant and we were playing the part of daffodils!' The other girls include Dorothy Hill, Janet Mooney, Janet Wilson and Betty –?. The boys are Bruce and Stanley. Stanley's parents, Edith and Stanley, both taught at Tinker's Farm.

Music in the hall at Trescott, *c.* 1946.

A nativity play at Trescott Infants' School, 1946. Brenda Daniels, née Gould, who supplied the photograph, is standing on the far right.

The nursery class at Trescott School, between 1941 and 1946. It is probably postwar, as there appears that little effort has been made to protect the glass roof.

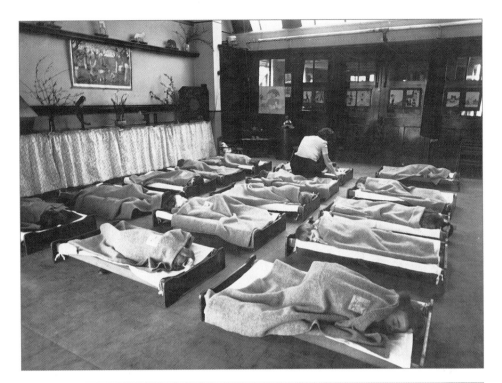

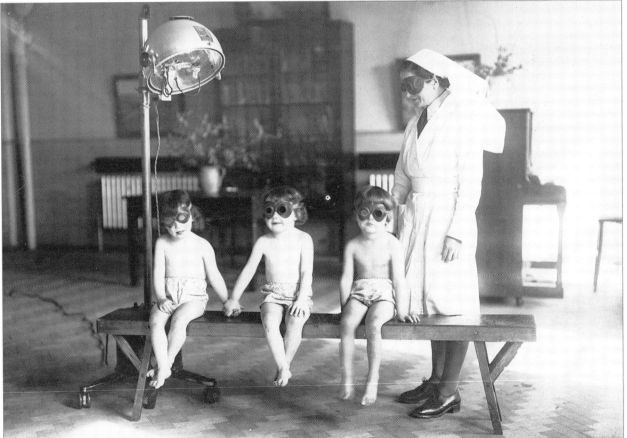

The sunray lamp in the school hall at Trescott School, *c.* 1946, was used to supplemement the children's vitamin D intake. Did it make them any healthier?

This page and opposite: Photographs taken during a nature walk by pupils from Trescott Infant School, 1949.

The school leaving age was increased to fifteen on 1 April 1947. The Tinker's Farm logbook reads: 'The staff was increased to meet the need occasioned by the implementation of the Education Act 1944 and forty girls of 14+ entered upon their fourth year at school. In addition forty-one were received from Colmer's Farm by reason of lack of accommodation on that site.' Later girls from Bartley Green were taken by coach each day to Tinker's Farm until the Bartley Green School opened in 1955.

Christmas nativity at Trescott Infant School, 1949.

An extract from *The Villa News & Record* of 1 May 1948, which refers to the forthcoming final of the Villa Cup, which was due to be played on the hallowed turf of Villa Park. In Northfield School's fiftieth anniversary booklet Bernard Dennington recalls: 'in the semi-final we beat Raddlebarn Road School in Selly Oak on a Saturday morning. They had two players who were already on Aston Villa's books. During the match I anticipated a back pass by Ray Spencer to the goalkeeper and nipped in to score. The excitement was tremendous. I was in another world! We led at half time and in the second half Howlett and Walters scored to make it 3–0'. The final was played on 5 May 1948 and the opponents, Loxton Street, ran out winners by three goals to nil. The team was as follows: M. Smith (goalkeeper), P. James (right back), D. Lacey (left back), D. Gould (right half), C. Sheppard (centre half and captain), G. Nichols (left half), B. Wooding (outside right), M. Howlett (inside right), B. Dennington (centre forward), G. Humphries (inside left) and ? Walters (outside left).

Tinker's Farm Boys' School, *c.* 1949. The photograph was supplied by Ernie Banks, who is on the left end of the second row. The pupils on the front row include F. Robinson, ? Pulfer, ? Guinan, B. Reynolds and B. Street. Those on the second row include E. Banks, D. Siddon, J. Savage, ? Nash and J. Mills. B. Goodenough and ? Potts are on the third row and F. Burrows, B. Mayo, J. Pym and A. Lowe are at the back. The teachers are Mr Wright, headmaster, and Mr Greenway.

A meeting of the Parent Teacher Association at Trescott, 1946. Two years earlier Trescott became the first school in Birmingham to set up a PTA. It came about after the close co-operation between home and school during the war years. A committee of twelve people was elected, initially under the chairmanship of headmistress Miss Kendall. There were two meetings a month, one of which was a talk and the other a whist drive, social or dance. A membership fee of 3*d* was suggested and surplus funds were used to provide vases for the hall, and a donation was given towards a sunray lamp for use in the nursery (see page 49).

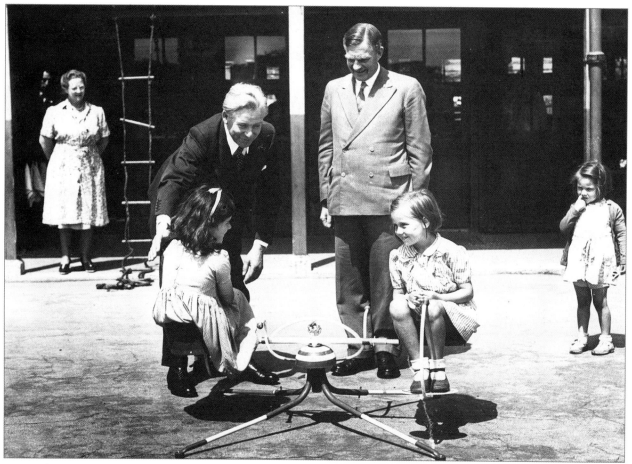

Mr Hardman MP and Sir Wilfred Martineau watch children at play with nursery toys at Trescott during at a meeting of the Federation of Parent Teacher Associations, Saturday 2 July 1949. Mr Hardman MP, Parliamentary Secretary to the Minister of Education, was the chief guest; 130 other people attended, including the Lord Mayor of Birmingham. Mr Hardman said: 'the parent's part in education is as important as the teacher's though in a different way. Only by cooperation between them – for which these associations provide opportunity – can the best results be obtained. The old idea of the teacher and parent in watertight compartments limits both.'

With the help of parental fundraising the nursery at Trescott was able to buy a D-Day landing craft, which, the school's records state, 'provides a constant source of enjoyment and recreation for the children: and it seems to us a far better use for such a vessel than its makers originally intended. Another piece of war equipment, which in our opinion, we have put to better use, is an RAF rubber dinghy, which again, the parents helped to buy, and which we inflate and use as a paddling pool. A set of nesting bridges has been a welcome addition to our large apparatus'.

Menu for one week.

Monday	Cheese Pie	Steamed pudding (plain)
	Parsley Sauce	Custard
	Peas	
Tuesday	Roast meat	Semolina
	Gravy	(Pink + chocolate)
	Cabbage,	
	Potatoes	
Wednesday	Stew	Steamed chocolate pudding
	Carrot	Custard
	Potatoe	
Thursday	Cottage Pie	Jam tart
	Peas	Custard
Friday	Boiled Fish	Blancmange
	Sauce	
	Potatoe	

Outdoor play on the veranda at Trescott Nursery, 1949. The school album states that the routine for three year olds included: 8.30 a.m. arrive, 9.15 a.m. hymn circle, 10.25 a.m. toilet, cod liver oil and milk, 10.45 a.m. indoor play, 12.00 dinner, 12.45 p.m. sleep, 1.15 p.m. story, 3.00 p.m. shoes on, fold blankets, 3.30 p.m. outdoor play, 4.15 p.m. go home. The school album, also details the menu for a typical week. Tuesday was the day to be off if you did not like chocolate semolina! A note alongside the menu list adds: 'Nursery children begin their mid-day meal with a rusk and finish it with a piece of raw carrot or square of cheese, when possible.'

Time for milk at
Trescott Nursery, 1949.

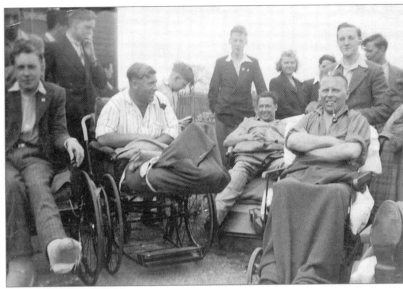

The Northcross Boys' Club, *c.* 1949. Ivan Parker recalls the team played at the ACCA ground. The team was supported by patients at the Cripples' Hospital and the matron is seen presenting medals to the team.

> 22.12.1949.
>
> I presented the leavers with their certificates this morning. The girls presented me with a writing case. Grace made a very happy speech on behalf of the school. We extended the assembly for a talk on Tinkers Farm past and future.
>
> Afternoon session closed early. We assembled to sing a Carol "To us a Child of Hope is born and "Jerusalem."
>
> We said "Good afternoon" many times and went home very slowly.
>
> I leave the school in the hands of my successor Miss A. V. Aston wishing her as much joy as I have had during my work here for the past eighteen years.
>
> Hilda R. Walmesley M.A
>
> (Retiring Headmistress.)

Miss Walmesley, the foundation headmistress at Tinker's Farm, retired at Christmas 1949. This is an extract from her final entry in the log book.

In the week of Miss Walmesley's retirement there was a presentation ceremony in the Assembly Hall. Miss Walmesley wrote: 'The old Queens and Scholars presented a very beautiful lectern and Bible to the school as a memento of my work as headmistress. Presentations were also made of personal gifts. It was a very memorable occasion and a happy one. The tone and spirit of the meeting was the greatest tribute of all and showed what their school life had meant to the girls. I felt and shall always feel deeply grateful.'

4
The 1950s

The Trescott Road estate, 1956. The school buildings are in the middle of the oval formed by
Norrington Road and Borrowdale Road.

JUVENILE DRAMATIC
1951
FESTIVAL
FESTIVAL OF BRITAIN EVENING

Chairman A.T. Goodborn Esq. B.Sc.

1. "The Contrary Mayor."   Dennis Road J.I.
(C. Constant)   Produced by Mr. G. Smith.

2. "Hansel and Gretel."   Grendon Road J.I.
(Grimm)   Produced by Mrs. M.J. Priestley.

3. "The Swineherd"   Trescott Road J.M.
(Hans Andersen)   Produced by Mr. H. Adams

4. "Rumpelstiltskin"   Lea Village J.M.
(Grimm - adapted) Produced by Miss D.A. Codling

Chairman's remarks - Interval.

5. "Midsummer Night's Dream."   Fentham Road S.M.G.

The 1951 Festival of Britain was one of the big events of the decade, and schools were involved in activities both in Birmingham and London. Trescott Road School took part in the Birmingham Schools' Festival of Britain Juvenile Dramatic Evening; two pupils from Tinker's Farm Girls' School, Thelma Harris and Janet Keeley, were in the choir that sang at the Royal Albert Hall during the London celebrations; and Tinker's Farm Infants held a festival concert that was held 'in spite of handicaps due to an epidemic of German measles and chicken pox'.

Pupils from Tinker's Farm at the Festival of Britain celebrations. The group includes Betty Smith, who was the 1950 May Queen, and her friend Josephine Laight, who are also pictured above (middle and right).

On 9 June 1951 there
was a 'Physical
Recreation & Dancing
Display' at Villa Park for
Her Royal Highness
Princess Elizabeth.
Miss Aslin was chief
marshall. A group from
Tinker's Farm Girls'
School performed
country dances.

A Coronation Open Day was held at Trescott on 20 May 1953, when maypole and country dancing were held in the playground watched by parents and friends of the school. Inside there were performances by the school choir and displays of work. The 'tasteful decorations in the hall were much admired, especially a model depicting the Coronation of Elizabeth I and a frieze portraying part of the present Coronation procession'. The afternoon ended with a Coronation service.

A Coronation party at Trescott, 1953. Notice the bunting all along the street.

As part of the Coronation festivities Miss Aslin
dedicated a bench to Tinker's Farm School.
The halls in the schools were used by the
whole estate for a party. The infant's school
logbook records that 'pupils have taken home
special Coronation handbook souvenirs of
wavers, crowns, parasols and windmills, and
they have each received a Coronation mug'.
Later in the month children visited Northfield
Picture House to see the Coronation film
Elizabeth is Queen.

Girls from Tinker's Farm visit St Paul's
Cathedral as part of their London tour on
16 June 1953, following in the footsteps of
the royal couple. After the Coronation holiday
Cllr Fisher visited the schools, and children
assembled for the dedication of stone-walled
seating which was placed around the oak
trees by the infant school.

Road safety lessons at Trescott, January 1953.

Trescott pupil Patricia Powell received this Road Safety Certificate in May 1954. Pupils also did drawings and coloured in road safety posters. Before the Second World War the Accident Prevention Council was known as the Birmingham Safety First Council. Messages on the back of school exercise books encouraged pupils 'for your own safety to learn by heart: Look both ways before crossing the road; Look both ways before passing in front or behind a standing vehicle; Never follow a rolling ball into the road or street: Always walk on the footpath, if there is one.' The message adds: 'many children are killed or seriously injured through neglecting to take care. Remember Safety First!'

1954

10th Sept.

Ley Hill Primary Junior and Infant School opened its doors to admit pupils for the first time on Tuesday, September 7th, 1954.

The teaching staff consisted of the following teachers.

Mr. D. E Wright, Headmaster,

Mrs. M. A. Lloyd, assistant, class 2, (6+ age group)

Mrs. B. P. Deykin, assistant, class 1, (5+ age group)

Miss M. E. Fielding, assistant, class 3, (7+ age group)

Mr. G. B. Whittle-Wills, assistant, class 5, (9+ and 10+ age groups)

Miss M. A. Wheeler, assistant, class 4, (8+ age group)

Miss B. E. Bishop, assistant, reception class.

A full meeting of the staff was held on the previous day, Monday, September 6th. At this meeting school organisation was laid down, record work books and schemes of work made available to the staff. Copies of the time table were put up in the Head's room and the staff room. The staff prepared their classrooms.

An enrolment of pupils had already been carried out in the presence of officers of the bye-laws department of the Education Committee on the previous Wednesday, September 1st.

By the end of the first week there were 106 pupils on the roll.

The opening page of the logbook of Ley Hill School indicates that it opened on 7 September 1954 under the leadership of Mr Wright. A 1960 report records: 'it was set up to serve a new estate to which families were being transferred from the heart of the city. Its building consists of eight classrooms and a hall'. The report added: 'the premises are pleasant and non-institutional in character.' The Tinker's Farm log book states that 'children from Allen's Cross estate are to be discouraged from attendance at Ley Hill as this school has been built in readiness for a new housing estate'. On its tenth anniversary Mr Wright recalled the site of the school: 'the hillside was still green meadowland, with cattle grazing on its upper slopes. But the hillside was about to be transformed. During the next ten years 1,600 children were going to receive their primary education at the bottom of the hill and most of their families were to find homes on the hillside.'

The first Trescott annual trip of the 1950s was to 'the Brummies Playground' at Weston-super-Mare. The school diary records: 'the morning was fine, and there was evidence of activity in the neighbourhood of the school as early as 7.30 am. By 8 o'clock, all those who were taking part in the adventure were ready, and soon afterwards the cavalcade set off – seven coaches, containing 212 children and 28 adults. The outward journey was via Evesham, the Cotswolds and Cheddar. Our time at Weston wasn't very long but every minute of it was enjoyed and full use was made of all the facilities offered, including the renowned Weston mud! It was a very memorable day in the annals of the school.'

The Trescott annual school visit in 1951 was to Rhyl. Eight coaches 'were very soon full with children armed with packets of sandwiches, and crates of milk. At five minutes past one, the coaches stood deserted – the invasion of the Marine Lake Pleasure Park had begun! Here in ideal surroundings, money was freely spent and thrills were plentiful. On the beach the donkeys were kept busy and the considerable amount of mud which had to be traversed did not prevent us from enjoying a paddle in the sea. We arrived home at 9.30 p.m. – weary, but very happy, after a most enjoyable day.'

The local community used the Tinker's Farm buildings for evening classes. Here, Betty Smith, centre, is joined by friends and neighbours ahead of an evening class in Pitman typing during 1953 or 1954. The work of the gardening classes is displayed in the background.

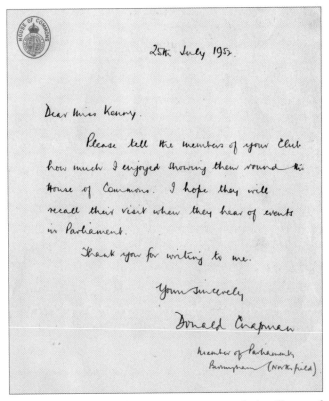

25th July 1952.

Dear Miss Kenny,

Please tell the members of your Club how much I enjoyed showing them round the House of Commons. I hope they will recall their visit when they hear of events in Parliament.

Thank you for writing to me.

Yours sincerely

Donald Chapman

Member of Parliament, Birmingham (Northfield)

Tinker's Farm Esperanto Club visited London in July 1952. A highlight of the visit was a tour of the House of Commons led by Donald Chapman, MP for Northfield. Following the visit the school received this letter from him.

At Trescott a dramatic festival was held on 14 July 1953. Over 200 parents and friends attended to see performances by every class. This was a performance of *The Mouse, the Frog, and the Little Red Hen*. The mouse was played by Carol Antrobus, the frog by Robert Cullen, the little red hen by Pamela Kilgour and Shirley Pugh and Kay Greathead were both heralds. At that time the school took part in numerous events including a performance of *Little Billie* at Oozells Street Juvenile Drama Festival.

Trescott School choir, 1952.

Trescott School staff, April 1956.
Back row, left to right: Beryl Beard, Huw 'Ted' Jones, Katie Williams, David Smith, Elizabeth Jones, Alan Edwards, Mrs Carlisle, Albert Houghton. *Front row*: Mrs Harding, the secretary, Miss Hemus, Denis Leach, deputy headmaster, Norah Huband, headmistress, Kay Williams, Jock Dick, Molly Lawson.

The Manor House,
Northfield,
Birmingham.

June, 1950.

The Girls of Tinkers Farm School.

Thank you very much for your kind message of congratulation and goodwill for my birthday: I have been most touched by the thoughts and kindliness of my many friends.

It was a very happy day: in the morning greetings from my family and friends, and in the afternoon a delightful time with hundreds of happy Bournville children and their parents at the annual Village Festival.

Eliz. Cadbury

Dame Elizabeth Cadbury sent this letter to the girls of Tinker's Farm School in June 1950 after children had sent their best wishes for her ninety-second birthday. Miss Aslin wrote in the school album that she was 'our good neighbour'. She was the wife of George Cadbury, son of the founder of the chocolate firm. She took a keen interest in the affairs of Tinker's Farm. On her death at the age of ninety-three the press said 'she had the art of identifying herself with whichever company she found herself in, and in speaking to the girls she invariably made them feel that she was one of them selves'. The Cadbury family was actively connected with the provision of the Allen's Cross Community Centre.

The Tinker's Farm stall at the United Nations Association fête and rally, held at Manor Farm on 16 June 1951. Pupils were involved in many activities which promoted active citizenship. Many took part in the 1950 Council for Education in World Citizenship conference.

A sea of faces as pupils listen to an Empire Day broadcast at Tinker's Farm Girls' School, 1951. Pupils include Audrey Thompson, Rita Instone, Alma Davies, Pauline and Jacqueline Parsonage, Pat Wallis, Margaret Wild, Gillian Randall, Christine Line, Joyce Rowe, Dena Woodhall and Rita Starling.

Tinkers Farm Girls' School's production of *Bluebird*, Christmas 1957. This was said to be 'an ambitious choice of Christmas entertainment but a successful one'. The basis of it is the search by two children, Tylfyl and Mytyl, for the bluebird of happiness. The presentation involved nine scene-changes and 162 girls appeared on stage. This scene is called 'The Kingdom of the Future'.

Harvest festival, Tinker's Farm Girls' School, 1959.

TINKER'S FARM OPERA GROUP

For the third summer in succession, the school has produced a Gilbert and Sullivan opera, the choice this year being "The Pirates of Penzance." So far as we know, we are the only Secondary Modern School in Birmingham which regularly Produces opera on this scale

From an educational point of veiw these productions have proved worth while, because quite a number of boys who have left school have formed an opratic society of their own which meets twice a week. A number of these old boys regularly attend professional and amateur performances given in the Birmingham district.

The fact that they have left school does not prevent our operatic old boys from taking an active interest in school productions, and our thanks go particularly to these old boys:

T. Battle, R. Young, D. Crow, A. Woolaston, R Skelding, M Burrows, M. Carrington, I. Carr, C. Fletcher, P. Guest, K. Harrison, B. Longstaffe, B. Lewthwaite.

For a number of boys in this last production, this is the fourth opera in which they have taken part. They are expecting talent scouts from D'Oyly Carte or Covent Garden any minute now.

We must admire the courage of the first and second year boys, who patiently submit to petticoats and bonnets. Some of them when in costume have been known to look prettier than their sisters, and parents have not been able to recognise this improved version of their offspring.

We must not forget to thank the Principals who gave freely of their time and skill, the orchestra. our scenepainter, electricians, carpenters and members of the staff who helped in many ways. And the boys themsevles - they came from 1A, 2A, 3A, 3B, 3C, and 4A. Class 3A have proved their worth again by providing us with pirates and girls.

Finally, our next production is to be "Trial by Jury". Let us hope that this will be even better than our previous successes.

J.S. J.T.

Left: The Tinker's Farm Chronicle, the Boys' School magazine, was first produced in July 1953. Mr Wright wrote: 'In presenting this first issue I hope you will keep it as a memory of your school days and refer to it many times in the years to come.' In the editorial D. Hardiman stated: 'these pages will show you that our school has achieved much during this past year and the magazine will be a lasting record of your school life'. *Above: The Tinker's Farm Chronicle* featured this lino print of a scene from *The Pirates of Penzance*, which was performed in 1953. The text states: 'so far as we know, we are the only Secondary Modern School in Birmingham, which regularly produces opera on this scale'. Other opera from this era included *HMS Pinafore*, *The Mikado* and *The Gondoliers*. A number of boys later went on to form the Tinker's Farm Opera Group. *Below*: Jimmy Taylor, middle of front row, is still with the opera.

Christmas at Trescott, 1946. The chief assistant, Mr Adams, adapted a fairy story, *Pot Luck* for the annual concert, which was called *The Princess and the Swineherd*. Pictured are Mr Adams, Ron Harrison, the prince, Lorna Phillips, the princess; Gary Bate, guard, Raymond Courtney, king. The press reported: 'it was a very gay affair, and Mr Adams' music had all its usual freshness and vitality'.

Staff at Trescott, *c.* 1958/9.

Girls at Tinker's Farm were taught domestic science in a fully furnished flat and kitchen, which was built in 1951. It became known as the Pastry Bowl. Previously midwifery classes were held at a house in Thorn Road, Bournville, where up to ten girls at a time spent a day making beds, cooking and washing. Here the hut forms the backdrop to a team photograph for the Torchbearers house team prior to the 1954 sports day.

Betty Howard, née Leake, on the far right, with her friends inside the Pastry Bowl in 1953 or 1954. This photograph was taken to commemorate the naming of the new building. Other pupils include Marilyn Lee, Diane Pardoe and Sylvia Venables. Betty is wearing one of the hats they wore during cookery lessons. The badge indicates that she is captain of the Invincibles house team.

CITY OF BIRMINGHAM EDUCATION COMMITTEE
Wheelers Lane SCHOOL Jm DEPT. 27.iv.1952

Dear Miss Huband,

I really must write you after our incomplete marathon football game to congratulate your boys on the splendid game they played on Saturday. It was the best Final Match that we have played in. I felt that the standard of play was remarkably good and the sportsmanship quite outstanding. There was not, I believe, the slightest suggestion of foul play throughout. Do tell your team how much we appreciated that.

Yours sincerely

The King's Norton & District shield is handed over to the captain of Trescott football team after the team had beaten Colmore Road in the 1951 Cup Final of the Kings Norton & District cup. The school log book records that the game was 'a fast one with the ball going from end to end and the result was in doubt until the final whistle. It was bad luck that Palmer, the captain, was ill in bed for this game. After 15 minutes, Wool scored the only goal of the match. The whole team played well, but the two backs, and particularly John Smith must be mentioned for an outstanding performance. Thus we bring the Shield back to Trescott for the second time. We have won it through sheer hard work on the part of the boys and their enthusiastic trainer Mr Pritchard'. He trained Trescott's boys for over twenty years.

This was a letter sent to the Trescott team in 1952 after they had played Wheeler's Lane School in the final of the Junior League Championship. 'Although extra time was played, the match ended in a goal-less draw, and so, for the second year in succession, we shared both the championship and Runners Up Shields with Wheelers Lane. It is said that a captain should always be an example to his side and that is what Colin Hoban has been this season. He has through sheer persistence been a thorn in the side of every defence we met'. During the season he scored six hat-tricks. 'Every boy played his part, not, it was felt, for personal glory, but for the honour of Trescott Road School'.

Trescott 1953/4. The diary states: 'although we relinquished the title of champions of junior section "A" of the Kings Norton and District Football League, we can say that the past season has been most successful. At the end of the season we finished runners up to Turves Green. Increasing the number of clubs playing in the league meant that we had to play eighteen games instead of our customary fourteen. Bad weather at the beginning of the year brought a congestion of fixtures towards the end of the season, but as a result of hurried telephone calls and frantic last minute rearrangements, we managed to complete our programme, with one day to spare. Of the eighteen league matches played, we won twelve, lost three and drew three. We scored a total of seventy goals whilst twenty-one were scored against us. . . . In the first round of the HMS Birmingham Shield, we travelled to Billesley Common to play Wheelers Lane. After a very exciting match, we lost by the only goal scored. Mention must be made of Reginald Clarke, a very popular captain, who set an example by his fine and constructive playing in many a match. Wing halves Brian Reaney and Norman Bates helped him to form a strong half back line. John Shepherd has had an excellent season as goalkeeper. His sound judgment and good sense of positioning saved many goals. He was undoubtedly one of the outstanding players in the team. In front of him at full back were Michael Harris and Phillip Hirons. Although liable sometimes to make mistakes, they both tried very hard at all times. David Pulling, in his second season with the team, played many good games at inside right. With twenty-five goals to his credit, he was third among the league goal scorers.

'Of the many boys tried at centre forward, Brian Stokes was the most successful. His dash and great determination helped him to score a number of goals. He obtained a great deal of help from inside left, Clifford Cushing, possibly the hardest worker in the team. Our two wingers, Alan Burrows and Peter Gould, although younger than the other boys, always gave a good account of themselves. As usual the reserves, Alan Bulmer, Barry Clynes and Kenneth Hubbard, were very reliable. Again, as in previous seasons, all the boys must be complimented for the fine team spirit and sense of sportsmanship that existed at every match throughout the season.'

Trescott's swimming champions of 1950 and 1951. The school's scrapbook proudly states: 'We are very proud to record that Helen Wallis has become the Champion Junior Girl swimmer of Birmingham.' Helen swam in the Annual Gala at Woodcock Street Baths on 20 October 1950 and won the championship. She received a medal and was presented, on behalf of the school, with a new bathing costume and cap, 'as a mark of our pleasure and pride in her splendid achievement'. The following year was the Centenary Gala of the Schools' Sports Federation and Brian Gregory of Trescott won a medal representing King's Norton & District. In November 1951 'excitement ran high' as Trescott won two district and one City trophy which was 'a feat unequalled by any other junior school in Birmingham'. Mr Dick and Mr James trained the children. Some of the 1951 girls are named. *Back row, left to right*: -?-, Brenda Gould. *Front Row*: Janet ?, Helen Wallis, Janet Higgins. The portrait on the left is of Helen Wallis.

The Tinker's Farm Boys' School football team twice played in the final of the Premier trophy, the Villa Cup at Villa Park. In 1948 the school lost 3–0 against Loxton Street School. The following season the Kings Norton District League was made up of boys from Tinker's Farm. In 1950/1 there was a memorable 15–0 win against Tennal School and the boys again reached the final, which was played against Aston Commercial at Villa Park. This article appeared in the *Villa News & Record*. It was an honour for the boys to play at Villa Park, even though the Villa was behind West Brom in the league at the time! In May 1951 the school log book record this entry written by headmaster Mr Wright: 'It is

worthy of note that the school has created various sporting records during the past year – the King's Norton School League, King's Norton Jubilee Shield and Joint Holders of the Villa Cup. As we won the Docker Shield in 1948 and the Fulford Athletics Shield in 1950 we have the distinction of having won all three premier trophies, a feat never before accomplished.' Captain John Bennett recalls the 1951 Villa Cup Final. 'We were all very thrilled to be running out onto the great Villa Park. Our opponents were Aston Commercial. They took the lead in the first half, but we drew level in the second half with a goal by Eric Pulfer. The final score was 1–1. The cup was shared. We tossed for the honour of holding the cup for the first six months, we won the toss and I was very proud to be presented with the cup in front of several thousand people'.

Left: Captain John Bennett, left, shakes hands with the captain of Aston Commercial School as the teams prepare to kick off the Villa Cup Final, 12 May 1951. *Above:* Headmaster Mr Wright shows off the Villa Cup with the help of R. Dixon, P. Mapother, E. Pulfer, M. Carrington, G. Smith and captain J. Bennett.

The victorious Tinker's Farm football team with the trophies they won in the 1950/1 season. The three trophies are the Kings Norton & District Shield, the Villa Cup and the Jubilee Shield. *Back row, left to right*: Gordon Smith, Michael Carrington, ? Briggs, Barry Mapother, John Baker, Roy Dixon, Reggie Nash, Eric Pulfer. Seated: John Pym, Mr Wright; headmaster, John Bennett; captain, Mr Blackmore, Maurice Burrows. Brian Chatwin and Frankie Butts are on the floor. Also of interest in this picture is the school organ which can be seen in the background. This is the only photograph that I've seen with the organ on it. Originally installed at Springfield College, Moseley, in 1866, the organ was removed to Rea Street, and following bomb damage to that school it was moved to Tinker's Farm in 1941 where it was first used in assembly on 20 November 1941. It had fifty silvered pipes and a light oak casing. Early in 1943 Mr Taylor composed the 'Tinker's Farm March'. Alderman Byng Kenrick officially inaugurated the organ and unveiled a huge mural on the hall wall, on 17 December 1941. The mural depicted Chaucer reading to characters from *Canterbury Tales*. The school logbook records that 'everyone seemed appreciative'. In 1961 the organ was 'extensively damaged'. A pupil at the school later 'admitted wrecking the organ' and was found guilty in court, fined and placed on probation. The organ was never used again.

A team photo of the Northcross Boys' football team, mid-1950s. Many of the boys were pupils at Tinker's Farm and are on the photograph above. *Back row, left to right*: -?-, Peter Keane, Gordon Smith, John Baker, -?-, John Roach, sadly the cloth-capped trainer's name is unknown. *Front row*: Patrick Mopather, John Bennett, ? Bradley, Brian Chatwin, Michael Carrington, Eric Pulfer.

Former Tinker's Farm teachers Mr Blackmore and Mr Ingley were guests of honour at the Northfield School fiftieth anniversary celebrations held in 1983. The large trophy is the Docker Shield, Birmingham's major cricket trophy donated by the Docker Brothers, former Warwickshire cricketers. They later owned a paint factory in Ladywood.

Tinker's Farm Boys' School won the prestigious Docker Shield in 1948, 1952 and 1955. Pictured is the team which won the Docker Shield on 18 July 1952. This team also became the Kings Norton League Champions. *Back row, left to right*: Frank Butts, David Hobbis, Ivan West, Keith Rose, Mr Ingley, John Roach, Malcolm Nicholls, Alan Maisey. *Front row*: Trevor Glover, Ronald Davis, Mr Wright, the headmaster, Roger Ottley, Terry Smith, John Leach. Teacher Norman Ingley, writing in *The Tinker's Farm Chronicle* stated: 'The 1952 team was the most outstanding team in the memory of cricket at Tinker's Farm losing only one match. It was a team of character and ability. They were a grand bunch and if they gave me some anxious moments they are also the only team I have ever framed so that I can preserve their memory for years to come.'

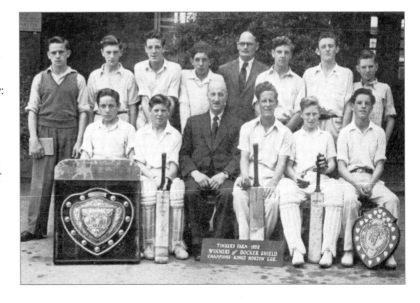

Sports day at Tinker's Farm
Girls' School, 1950: the first
year skipping race.

Sports day, 1952: the 'catch the
train' race.

Tinker's Farm girls get the sack
at the sports day, 1952.

All lined up and ready not to go! Another 1952 sports day photograph showing the 'slow bicycle race', where the aim was not to come first!

Miss Aslin presents the winner's shield to Joan Mernagh at sports day, 1952.

The Tinker's Farm Girls Senior Relay team, at the King's Norton & District Sports, 1956. *Left to right*: K. Dormiss, Pat Gee, Brenda Nesbitt and Pauline Rogers.

The Tinker's Farm team that won the King's Norton and District Netball Shield in 1957. *Back row, left to right*: Miss Chappell, mistress, Miss Aslin, headmistress, Pat Collins, Mrs Banbury, mistress. *Middle row*: Carol Hartill, Maureen Adams, Pat Gee, Brenda Nesbitt, Judith Jackson. *Front row*: Pat Heath and Ursula Moore. Besides those eight girls a number of other girls also played in the championship: these were Pauline Rogers, Janet Perry, Jeanette Lowe, Jacqueline Morris and Valerie Bradbury. The girls also achieved success in other sports, most notably Pat Gee, the head girl of the school, who ran for Birchfield Harriers Juniors at the White City; Brenda Nesbitt, who also represented the district sports teams; and Pat Collins who was the Warwickshire Intermediate High Jump Champion.

Betty Smith is crowned the 1950 May Queen.

Scenes from the Tinker's Farm's May Festival, 1950. This is Form 4 performing *Clerk of the Weather*. Hazel Parker is on the back row next to the cockerel!

The 1951 May Festival at Tinkers Farm Girls' School that saw Valerie Bennett crowned. Valerie and Shirley Hall represented the school in Victoria Square to hear the proclamation ceremony following the death of King George VI in 1952.

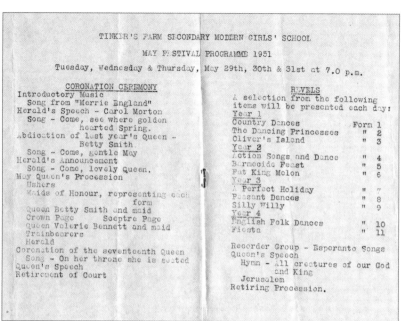

TINKER'S FARM SECONDARY MODERN GIRLS' SCHOOL

MAY FESTIVAL PROGRAMME 1951

Tuesday, Wednesday & Thursday, May 29th, 30th & 31st at 7.0 p.m.

CORONATION CEREMONY

Introductory Music
   Song from "Merrie England"
Herald's Speech - Carol Morton
   Song - Come, see where golden
       hearted Spring.
Abdication of last year's Queen -
       Betty Smith
   Song - Come, gentle May
Herald's Announcement
   Song - Come, lovely Queen.
May Queen's Procession
   Ushers
   Maids of Honour, representing each
       form
   Queen Betty Smith and maid
   Crown Page   Sceptre Page
   Queen Valerie Bennett and maid
   Trainbearers
   Herald
   Coronation of the seventeenth Queen
   Song - On her throne she is seated
Queen's Speech
Retirement of Court

REVELS

A selection from the following
items will be presented each day:

Year 1
Country Dances   Form 1
The Dancing Princesses   " 2
Oliver's Island   " 3
Year 2
Action Songs and Dance   " 4
Barmecide Feast   " 5
Fat King Melon   " 6
Year 3
A Perfect Holiday   " 7
Peasant Dances   " 8
Silly Willy   " 9
Year 4
English Folk Dances   " 10
Fiesta   " 11

Recorder Group - Esperanto Songs
Queen's Speech
   Hymn - All creatures of our God
      and King
   Jerusalem
Retiring Procession.

The May Festival programme featured a hand-coloured cover.

From the 1951 May Festival programme.

Form 8 performs national dances at the 1952 May Festival.

The 1953 May Queen Diane Davis and her consorts.

The recorder group performs at the 1953 May Festival at Tinker's Farm Girls' School.

The May Festival, 1954. May Queen Norma Croft and her consorts in the playground, watched by pupils from the neighbouring junior and infant schools.

The Small Court at the 1955 May Festival: Queen Norma and Queen Diana with Herald Jacqueline Joy. The Crown Page was Dawn Stewardson; the Sceptre Page was Ann Stokes. The three ushers are Margaret Corey, Sheila Smith and Audrey Talbot.

With the old face of Northfield rapidly disappearing beneath a mask of bricks and mortar—and however much one may sigh for green fields and Greener Belts, the fact remains that people have got to be housed somewhere—the annual May Festival at Tinker's Farm Girls Secondary Modern School serves more and more as a reminder of the Northfield that once was. Listening, at Tuesday's ceremony, to the School Herald declaiming that on this very spot the apple blossom once flourished, one realised almost with a shock that this was no flight of whimsical fancy. The School in truth does stand in what was once an orchard. On equally safe historical ground is the assertion that the flames of tinkers' fires once glowed in the neighbourhood. It is an excellent thing, one felt, that this continuity with the past should have been preserved from the very beginning when the authorities agreed to the name "Tinker's Farm" instead of their original suggestion of "Kelby Close School." Not only did they anticipate, by twenty-odd years, a decision of the Ministry of Education that names of schools should be a little more imaginative than that of the road or district in which they happened to be, but they kept the faith with tradition. A many-splendoured thing, in the modern idiom.

The visitors who watched Queen Diane Merryweather crown her successor, Queen Patricia Gee, in a ceremony which seemed even more intense than usual, included Anglican Roman Catholic and Free Church clergy, civic representatives and teachers from other schools. The Herald was Marlene Pike, Barbara Aldridge was Crown Page, and the duties of Sceptre Page were shared by Pat Hargreaves and Pauline Rogers. The attendant maids were Hilda Polson (for Diane) and Margaret Moss (for Pat); the train-bearers Pat McKeever and Pamela Bates; and the ushers Christine Bridges, Ann Benton and Sylvi Bakewell. Flower maids were Jacqueline Joy, Valerie Winter, Wendy Davies, Susan Hadfield, Susan Starling, Dorothy Hodgkiss, Mavis Hadley, Brenda Nesbitt, Christine Mills and Pat Polson.

A notable feature of the revels this year was the high standard of the country dancing, particularly in the intricate Fandango, which, despite its name, is English. Among the sketches, there was some outstanding work in a nineteenth century comedy, "The Spinsters of Lushe"; "A Quiet Tea Party" provided ten minutes of sheer hilarity; and the Americanisms of the younger sister in "Grand Partiality" were extremely entertaining. There was some intelligent miming in a version of "Ceres and Persophene"; the quality of the costumes in "The Imp Tree" was very high and there was a delightful Chinese play, "The Stolen Prince."

Patricia Gee was crowned May Queen in 1956. This article appeared in the local press. In her album Miss Aslin wrote 'so true' next to the opening paragraph.

Susan Starling is crowned the 1957 May Queen. She
is pictured here with retiring May Queen Pat Gee.

Susan Starling in the early 1980s, when she
responded to the request to help Northfield
School's fiftieth anniversary celebrations. She
is pictured in Bermuda where she worked in
a hotel.

Pat McKeever was the 1958 May Queen – elected 'with due pomp and pageantry'. The local press
reported: 'there was no teacher who did not contribute a share to the spectacle that was interesting, and
it all made for a spectacle that was interesting, educational and at times rather moving'. The Full Court
is pictured here in the school garden.

The final May Festival at Tinker's Farm Girls' School was held in 1959. May Queen Glenda Pike was crowned before a packed hall. A festival of this kind, Miss Aslin declared, 'promoted a spirit of well being, character, and leadership among the pupils, and such qualities we wish to have in our school'. The ceremony began with a song from *Merrie England* and then the Herald, Betty Gormley, delivered her speech. The abdication of Pat McKeever, the previous year's May Queen, was said by the local press to be 'a most impressive sight', and she 'gave of her best with a poise which would have done credit to a seasoned performer'.

Typing to music at the 1959 May Festival celebrations.

June 6th 1957. Today has been the last day, in this building, of this Infants' School — The Secondary Modern Girls' School takes over the whole block & the Boys Sec. Mod. S will occupy the Junior School buildings. To bring about this reorganisation, a new Primary School has been built, to be known as "Bellfield School. All staff will attend tomorrow to

Extract from the school logbook of June 1957. This refers to the final day of Tinker's Farm Infant School before the move into the new building, which was to be called Bellfield School.

One of the first class photographs taken at Bellfield School, 1957.

The opening of Bellfield was designed to free the whole of the accommodation at Tinker's Farm for Secondary School use, in order to meet the increasing demand for secondary-school accommodation arising from housing development in the vicinity. An annexe on Frankley Beeches Road, used by Tinker's Farm Infants' School was closed and taken over by St Brigid's School. The logbook states: 'all staff will attend tomorrow to assist in transferring stock, stores and apparatus. The children of the primary departments will not be in attendance. About ten children have withdrawn on account of the longer distance to travel. The staff has worked well and cheerfully, in order to make the move and we have willing help from our girls and boys schools.'

The following day the headmistress wrote: 'I went to Bellfield School at 8.00 a.m. and found the classrooms unready for occupation, the entrance hall sealed off, so that the floor machine could operate, and no stockrooms available. It was 6.00 p.m. before the vans departed and left goods and packages scattered around. The staff volunteered to come during the Whitsun holiday to prepare for the opening of Bellfield on June 7th. It was an exhausting and frustrating day as we said farewell to Tinker's Farm Primary Infants' School, after the twenty years of its existence.'

The new junior and infants school was opened on 7 June 1957, although the official opening ceremony was not held 15 October 1957. The former prime minister, Clement Attlee, performed the opening ceremony. The local press reported: 'Most of the children had a holiday today for the official opening. The remainder, about 100 juniors and 40 infants gathered with their parents at the schools to welcome the visitor. A short service of dedication was followed by a speech by Earl Attlee. Headmistress of the Infant School Miss Farrow and Headmaster of the Junior School Mr H. Green then took Clement Attlee on a tour of the buildings. After the tour the National Anthem was sung.'

The junior school entrance hall, pictured in a brochure printed to commemorate the official opening in 1957. The brochure stated that the school was a three-form entry school; the junior school could accommodate 480 pupils in 12 classes.

A junior classroom. The local press made much of the bright colour scheme of the school stating that one classroom has 'a sky blue floor with two of the walls painted grey, a third wall cyclamen pink and the fourth, lemon yellow'. This contrasted sharply with the 'deplorable' old schools in the inner city built by the Victorians with 'great affection for brown paint'.

The Bellfield Infant assembly hall, 1957. The infant school was designed to accommodate 360 pupils in nine classes. The official brochure refers to the building 'being on a site which falls very steeply into the north corner. Good views across to Ley Hill and Bartley Green wooded slopes are obtained, and the buildings have deliberately been planned on the steepest part of the site so that flatter areas may be used for play areas'.

5
The 1960s

Jean Morton, of 'Tingha & Tucker' fame, was the ajudicator at the 1964 Tinker's Farm Poetry Festival, and is seen here with Mrs Morris.

In November 1961 Tinker's Farm Girls' School held its first Speech Day, which replaced the traditional, but by then outdated May Festivals. Mrs Laurence Cadbury chaired the inaugural event. Pictured are Pamela Kilgour and Kathlyn Chawner, who was head girl, Miss Aslin, the headmistress, Mrs Cadbury, Miss Walmesley and Cllr Mrs Doris Fisher, who was later to chair the first Boys' Speech Day in November 1963. The change over from May Festival to Speech Day 'proved to be an auspicious and successful occasion' which was attended by several hundred people. Miss Aslin spoke of the school's continued success in international affairs, of the success of the athletics team and the need for pupils to continue to receive 'the utmost support and encouragement from home, the church, youth club and welfare organizations, together with some guidance for living, preferably by example from adults'.

PRIZES 1960-1
FORM PRIZES FOR ATTAINMENT OR SPECIAL EFFORT

First Year
Sonia Moore	Christine Harborne	Marion Jones
Susan Spier	Maureen Rodgers	Pamela Bishop
Sandra Owen	Sandra Langman	

Second Year
Sandra Hargreaves	Denise Bowman	Susan Cherry
Roberta Merryman	Joyce Roberts	Sandra Hoban
Barbara James	Peggy Fisher	

Third Year
Valerie Dipple	Patricia Taylor	Sonia Slater
Carole Doleman	Rita Haddock	Gillian Clay
Valerie Wintle	Shirley Crawford	

Fourth Year
Janet Carter	Sandra Harlow	June Sweet
Frances Smith	Suzanne Delahay	Anita England

Fifth Year
Christine Pittam

COMMERCIAL COURSE CERTIFICATES
Pitman's Examination Institute
SHORTHAND

	Maximum Speed Attained
Janice Sumner	60 words per minute
Linda Ashfield	70 ,, ,, ,,
Susan Clay	80 ,, ,, ,,
Gillian Garner	80 ,, ,, ,,
Carole Robinson	80 ,, ,, ,,
Glynis Llewelyn	80 ,, ,, ,,
(Frances) Ann Mellor	90 ,, ,, ,,
Barbara Swain	90 ,, ,, ,,
Sandra Warlow	90 ,, ,, ,,
Christine Pittam	100 ,, ,, ,,

SPECIAL AWARDS

PRESENT HEAD GIRLS' PRIZE

Kathlyn Chawner

SERVICE TO THE SCHOOL (PREFECTS)

Georgina Bennett

Joy Wright

SPORTS SHIELD TROPHY

WON BY PIONEERS

Captain: Sandra Harlow

POETRY FESTIVAL

(Picture presented by COUNCILLOR MRS. FISHER)

Won by: Upper School, Form 3(1)

Lower School, Form 1(3)

Some of the prizewinners for 1960/1 taken from the programme of events.

The fourth Girls' School Speech Day, which was held on 18 November 1964. Frank Butler (left), headmaster of the Boys' School, chaired the event. The other gentleman is Mr H. Barlow of King's Norton Secondary School.

The audience at the Speech Day, 1964. The pupils at either end of the front row are Christine Hebron and Angela Cash.

The group of dignitaries who attended the eighth and final speech day at Tinker's Farm Girls' School, 1968. The adults on the back row are Miss Chesterton and Mr Morgan, the deputy headmaster. On the front are the three headmistresses of the school, Miss Aslin (headmistress 1950–67), Mrs Betty Kendall (the acting headmistress), Miss Walmesley (headmistress 1931–49). The head girl is Susan Wheeldon. Miss Walmesley spoke of the traditions of the school which 'should be forwarded to produce a strong promise of future development in the new school; to make worth while the ideals for which comprehensive education was planned'.

An extract from the Tinker's Farm Boys' School Speech day booklet from November 1965. Prizes were given by Mr A. Davies, the education and training officer of Cadbury Brothers. The award for Champion House for good work and conduct went to the Saxons. The Britons won the swimming cup; the Danes won the athletic cup and the cross-country cup. The Normans won the football knockout competition. At the previous year's Speech Day the headmaster, Mr Butler, said: 'there is a danger that in our day-to-day attempt to instill knowledge into a boy we may lose sight of the ultimate aim. In my opinion this is to procure a well balanced mind, capable of reasoning, and searching for truth, to aim at integrity and honesty.' The school inspector, Mr Hey, said: 'Anyone who had connections with the Austin firm would know that computer machines were capable of working millions of times faster than man. A speed up by tens of millions of times, was just around the corner and tremendous change was coming in the next ten years, As the industrial revolution had knocked out the unskilled worker by hand, so would the computer put the untrained mind out of action.'

House Awards

CHAMPION HOUSE (Work, Conduct, etc.):

SAXONS

SWIMMING CUP awarded at Swimming Gala:

BRITONS

ATHLETIC CUP awarded on Sports Day:

DANES

FOOTBALL (Knock-out Competition):

NORMANS

CROSS-COUNTRY CUP:

DANES

P95970 (a) 109/33

6

The school library at Trescott, 1961. This was housed in one of the huts in the playground. One of two air-raid shelters can be seen in the background.

Recorders at Trescott, 1961.

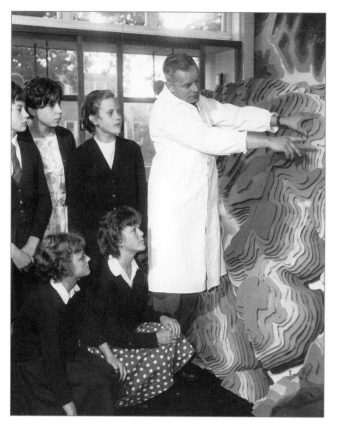

Mr Holliday, the science master at Tinker's Farm, with a group of third-year girls, shows a large contour model of the Elan Valley that he made. It was used in lessons and exhibited at a fair in September 1963 at Birmingham University. It was made as a relief map and accurately showed the 50 ft contours which the local press said, 'gives a startling picture of the configuration of the ground'.

Pupils made regular trips to the Elan Valley and the Frankley water works. Here first-year pupils inspect the Elan Valley complex on an organised trip in 1964.

Staff from Tinker's Farm Boys' School in front of the greenhouse, mid- to late 1960s. Boys tended the greenhouse behind the caretaker's house off Tinker's Farm Road. In 1965 they gained many awards at the King's Norton and West District Horticultural Exhibition. Mr Gasking was the exhibition secretary.

The staff at Tinker's Farm Girls' School, c. 1966. *Front row, left to right*: Mr Morgan, Mrs Taylor, Mrs Belton, Mrs Thompson, Mrs Kendall, Miss Aslin, Mrs Brookes, Mrs White, Mrs Hackney, Miss Curtis and Mr Holiday. The back row includes Miss Kempson, Mrs Collins, Miss Scott and Miss Rollason.

Christmas at Tinker's Farm, 1961.

Mrs Trigg and form 4.2 on a trip to London, 1962.

A performance of *A Midsummer Night's Dream* at Tinker's Farm, July 1962. Three of the girls are Joy Teall (head girl 1963/4), Pat Taylor (head girl 1962/3), Pamela Kilgour (head girl 1961/2). The song 'Ye Spotted Snakes' was performed by Forms 3.4 and 3.3.

A performance of *A Midsummer Night's Dream* at Tinker's Farm, July 1964. Here Titania, played by Beryl Sweet, is with the fairies. The local press said: 'An outstanding feature of the play was the costumes, many of which were positively lavish.' In 1966 Mr Morgan produced a 'very colourfully dressed presentation of *The Spinsters of Lushe*.

Mrs Dain conducts Form 2.3, winners of the lower-school prize at the Poetry Festival, 1964. The Upper School winners were Form 4.1.

Trescott's cricket team with teacher Pete Davies, mid-1960s.

A photograph of the Trescott football team and a handwritten report of the season, from the school scrapbook, written by an unnamed pupil, 1959/60. In 1960 the English Schools Football Association awarded Football Proficiency Certificates to John Mortimer, Raymond Smith, Douglas Browning and Kenneth Linnecor. The following year Kevin Parsonage, John Stevens, Stephen Rowles and Trevor Boyce also passed the scheme. 'They were tested at Northfield Park, kicking with left and right foot, passing, dribbling, heading, throw-ins, and kicking goalwards. There was also a special test according to the position of the player and questions on the rules.' At that time Mr Gasking of Tinker's Farm Boys' School was the treasurer of the Kings Norton & District FA.

Trescott Football Team

The above team played in the II Div. of the Kings Norton District. We entered for the Kalamazoo Shield and the H.M.S Birmingham Cup. Altogether we played 17 matches. Won 6, drew 3 and lost 9 x 8. Kenneth Linnecor our centre forward was top goal scorer

Team
G.K
T. PLUMB

R.B   L.B
K. PARSONAGE   GARRATT

R.H   C.H.   L.H
DANIELS   LEE   SILVESTER

            IR   IL
OR   SMITH   C.F.   BUTTS   OL
MORTIMER   LINNECOR   BROWNING

Trescott swimmers, 1961. Pictured are John Feeney and Lynne Thompson who won the diving shield at the swimming gala, which was held at Tiverton Road baths in June.

The 1967/8 skittleball team at Trescott School. Skittleball was particularly popular in the 1960s. In 1960 the school's scrapbook records 'the team trained by Miss Morris and Mrs Edwards had a very successful season. Although they only lost two matches during the season they could only manage to be runners up in the league. A very good season – well done girls.' The 1961 skittleball captain was Janet Steadman.

PE display at Trescott, 1961. Terence Mosedale wrote in the scrapbook: 'In our PE Display there were 24 children, our girls were very good they did some caterpillars. One of our girls whose name is Anita Grant did some spectacular things. I stood on my head and Raymond Spotswood, David Baker and Barrie Smith dived over me. Anne McGough went on the apparatus and did our grand finale. We did it in front of the parents on Parents Day.' Pictured going over the box (right) is Gillian Davies, supported by Anita Grant and Deborah Stanley. *Bottom right*: Barbara Tilson, Sheila Matthews, Dorothy Yates and Linda Bateman working in a group with a ball and hoops. *Bottom left*: David Baker, Geoffrey Bridge, Terry Mosedale and Malcolm Jones on the climbing frames.

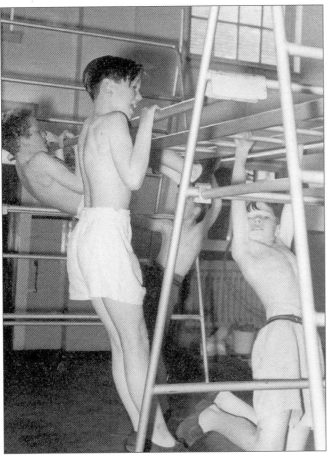

Ley Hill School football team, *c.* 1964. *Back row, left to right*: Mark Hayward, Rob Moore, Terry James, Norman Pemberton, Keith Dunn. *Front row*: Ronnie Moore, -?-, -?-, Chris Ray, Lee Evans, Norman Gilbert.

Ley Hill's skittleball team, 1968.

Running for home in the Ley Hill Infants' flat race, run over 40 yards, June 1968 are Marie Prothero, Jackie O'Keefe, Carol Thompson, Jenny Jones and Carol Puttam. The first annual sports day, organised by Mr Smith, was held in May 1958.

Sporting success at Bellfield, 1968. David Settle on the far right shows off a swimming trophy to team mates and headmaster Mr Green.

Tinker's Farm Boys' School football team, 1964. They were the Intermediate Champions of their division. Headmaster Mr Butler is at the back far left.

Tinker's Farm cricket team, 1966.

The presentation to Miss Chesterton upon her retirement as deputy headmistress at Tinker's Farm Girls' School, July 1963. *Left to right*: Mr C. Hey, the district inspector, Miss Aslin, headmistress, Miss Chesterton, Cllr Doris Fisher, Miss Walmesley, former headmistress, Miss Farrow, former infants' headmistress. Miss Chesterton, who went to Tinker's Farm in 1932 to take charge of the science laboratory. She was later instrumental in setting up the BBC broadcasts for schools, and she was deputy headmistress at the time of her retirement. She was presented with a gold watch, a thermometer, plants for her greenhouse and a linen tablecloth. Miss Chesterton passed away in August 1982.

Teacher Sue Kitchin, later Mrs Hazzard, conducts the Tinker's Farm choir at the 1969 Speech Day.

Miss Aslin, headmistress at Tinker's Farm Girls' School from January 1950, retired at the end of the summer term in 1967. The Chief Education Officer, Sir Lionel Russell, paid tribute to her 'wonderful, splendid record of valuable and devoted work in the city'. He added, 'there must be countless women who in their heart of hearts must feel a debt of gratitude to her.' She was presented with a tea maker, a radio and an electric kettle by deputy headmistress Betty Kendall on behalf of the staff and education colleagues. Frank Butler, the headmaster at the boys' school, announced his retirement at the same time and the decision was taken to merge the two schools into one at the earliest opportunity. The deputy headteachers of the respective schools, Mrs Kendall and Mr Purser, became acting headteachers at the schools until they closed at the end of the summer term in 1969. Northfield Comprehensive School, taking the boys and girls from the former schools, opened in the same buildings under the leadership of Laurie Green in September 1969, pictured in the middle of the front row of this Northfield Comprehensive School staff photograph taken in 1969/70 academic year. The full list of names includes Lesley Tittle, John Robertson, Don ?, Roger Sturman, Dave Henry, Cedric Lee, Harry Fides, Diane Jakeway, Nev McFarlane, Ray Davis, Mr Bonner, Mr Malpass, Sam Doble, Doc Holiday, Mike Hendly, Margaret Smith, Mary Bosson, Cath Curtiss, Mrs Robertson, Mr Morgan, Mr Pollard, Mr Lawson, Mr Green (headmaster), Paddy Leeson, Tom Thomas, Mrs Belton and Mr Fulton.

6
The 1970s

The Queen's Silver Jubilee celebrations at Bellfield Infant School, 1977.

Left: Bellfield Infants' School held a celebration of the Queen's Silver Jubilee on 25 May 1977. This booklet was produced detailing the occasion, which started with a prayer from the Revd Mr Ward and ended with 'God Save the Queen'. *Right:* A street-style Jubilee party was held in the playground at Bellfield School.

Classes at Bellfield School created special Jubilee displays and decorations, and pupils dressed in various costumes.

Above, left: A guardsman attended Trescott School to hand out Jubilee coins in honour of the Queen's twenty-five-year reign. Five-year-old Sharon Mellon is seen proudly clutching her coin after receiving it on stage in the school hall from Irish guardsman Paddy McGuire. Sharon recalls: 'in the build up there was lots of excitement and everyone was really looking forward to it. On the day there was a great atmosphere.' The object in the top left-hand corner is part of a Jubilee crown that was suspended from the ceiling. *Above right:* Bellfield School had a special guest for their Jubilee celebrations, Sergeant Robinson of the 1st Battalion Grenadier Guards. He told pupils of his royal duties, which included guarding Buckingham Palace and the Tower of London. The pupils were presented with Jubilee medals and sang a special tune, 'The Guard and the Palace Gate'.

The Jubilee street party in Porlock Crescent.

A great photograph of local people celebrating the Jubilee – sorry, no names, but it probably shows staff and customers of the Highlander pub, as Fourlands Road off Merritts Hill is in the background.

The whole school entered a Christmas hat competition at Ley Hill in 1970. The logbook records: 'there were many splendid entries and the children provided an entertainment on the last afternoon. Hilarious!'

A staff photograph at Ley Hill School, c. 1971. *Back row, left to right*: Sheila Swann, Gaye Hadley, Mary Blackhall. *Front row*: Nancy Kerr, Judy Thompson, Anona Easterby, Rhoda Rowlands.

LANES 1	2	3	4	5	6
FH	LD	NT	FH	LD	NT

BREAST STROKE

LANES 1 FH	2 LD	3 NT	4 FH	5 LD	6 NT
EVENT 9 - 1st Year Girls					
J.Quigley	M.Morton	S.Stephenson	B.Casey	D.Butler	J.Thomas
EVENT 10 - 1st Year Boys					
W.Harrison	I. Jones	G. Bolus	S.Humphries	D.Simpkins	R. Egan
EVENT 11 - 2nd Year Girls					
S.Button	S.Williams	W.Jones	S.Bullock	D.Parkes	D.Norris
EVENT 12 - 2nd Year Boys					
R.Pickering	M.Babbington	L.Shakles	R.Hall	R.Knowles	S.Jones
EVENT 13 - 3rd Year Girls					
W.Taylor	J.Genockey	J.Taylor	M.Genockey	S.Badger	S.Leslie
EVENT 14 - 3rd Year Boys					
P. Gough	K.Shipley	P.Rose	J.Thompson	M.Edwards	J.Loverid
EVENT 15 - 4th Year Girls					
S.Jones		C.Hall	C.Jones		B.Genock
EVENT 16 - 4th Year Boys					
P.Madden	M.Jennings	G.Mullis	P.Hickman	P.Powell	C.Shirley

- 3 -

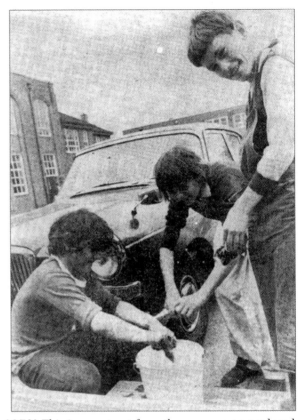

Above, left: How many of these names can you recognise from 1973? This is an extract from the programme produced for Northfield School's swimming gala in July 1973. The gala was held at Woodcock Street Baths. *Right:* Pupils Keith Wood, Jimmy Harrison and Patrick O'Connor car washing at Northfield School to raise funds for a school minibus, May 1974. The local press stated the pupils and PTA had 'thrown themselves wholeheartedly' into the fundraising, 'giving enormous enthusiasm and support'.

A further fundraising effort at Northfield School raised about £400 when a fashion show was held as part of the fayre in 1974. Ray Carter, MP for Northfield, attended and spoke to pupils. *Left to right*: Susan Heyes, Janet Bird, Susan Davies, Lynn Gardner and Lynne Floyd.

Northfield School forged links with feeder schools in the area. Here Elizabeth Poole and Paul Purvin of Northfield School show off a number of toys made pupils at Northfield. These were presented to youngsters at the Meadows School. The toys included aeroplanes, trucks, carts and scooters. Pictured with them are Northfield School's new headmaster Mike Evanson and teacher John Broomfield.

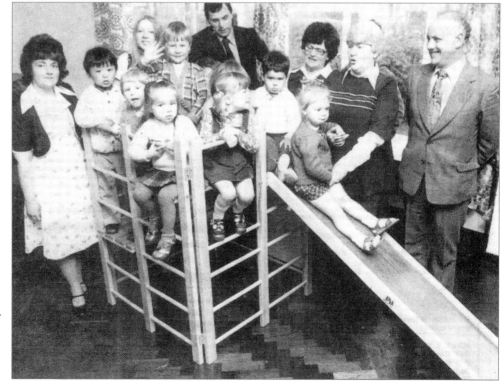

Northfield School linked up with local play schemes. On the right are Betty Howard, leader of the Westcote Hall playgroup, and Tony Babbington, chairman of Northfield School PTA. The new equipment was paid for in part by the PTA. The girl on the slide is two-year-old Lesley Stone.

Trescott Junior School's Skittleball team, December 1977. *Back row, left to right*: Amelia Shaw, Charlotte Donnelly, Lorna Hegenbarth, Elaine Neill, Miss Bird, Joanne Anderton, Phoebe Evans, Jayne Aston, Sharon Breeze. *Front row*: Sharon Harris, Begum Cameron, -?-, Theresa Oakley, Sally Ann Ward, Rhoda Paul, Sharon Sorrell.

Northfield Reds FC, that trained in the Northfield School gym, show off its cup won in the 1977/8 season. *Back row, left to right*: Dennis Howard, manager, Pete Powell, Phil Harrison, Gary Thatcher, Billy Smith, Keith Aldridge, Micky Reeves, Ian Wainwright, the youth worker. *Front row*: Steve Neil, Phil Fowler, Ray Howard, Jimmy Rainsford, and John Loveridge. All were eighteen or nineteen years of age.

Footballers from Ley Hill School with teacher Peter Wylde, 1978. The pupils include Mark Joye and Dean Palmer.

Cliff Mitchell, who was in charge of the library at Northfield School. The five pupils are assumed to be librarians. This photograph was taken between 1970 and 1972, as the pupils are wearing the original school badge which had a large N and C, standing for Northfield Comprehensive School. Comprehensive education was all the vogue at the time. The badge was later altered when the school dropped the word comprehensive from the title, and proudly became Northfield School.

Northfield School pupils at work in the new craft block that provided woodworking and auto engineering facilities that were the envy of other secondary schools. Work began on the block on 14 May 1979. The opening of it was overshadowed by the death, the previous month, of Cllr Neil Scrimshaw, who had worked tirelessly to promote the school. The school's logbook records: 'no man has done more for this school than Cllr Scrimshaw – all the improvements that have taken place are due to his drive and support. I had hoped that he would open the craft block.' Mrs Margaret Scrimshaw officially opened it in November 1980.

Northfield School pupils at work helping to improve the school gardens. The horticultural work was greatly enhanced by the greenhouse, which was on the land behind the caretaker's house on the Tinker's Farm Road side of the school. This can be seen on page 99. There is no indication of when these were taken, some people have suggested the boys were Tinker's Farm pupils, but it seems more likely that they were pupils from the early days of Northfield School, not in school uniform because of their gardening work.

A Northfield School football team with teacher Mike Hendley who was Head of languages, mid-1970s.

A football team at Northfield School with teacher Steve Allatt, mid-1970s.

Geography teacher Andy Lamb with his football team, Northfield School, mid-1970s.

Football at Northfield School, mid-1970s. The teacher is Ian Wainwright.

Teacher Roger Sturman with his football team at Northfield School, mid-1970s.

Teachers Yvonne Whetton (left) and Sue Williams with one of Northfield School's netball teams, mid-1970s.

Hockey at Northfield School, mid-1970s.

Sam Doble with one of his basketball teams from Northfield School.

Rugby at Northfield School, mid-1970s.
The teacher is Sam Doble.

Head of PE at Northfield School was the
ever-popular England rugby player Sam
Doble. He represented Moseley, North
Midlands and England at rugby football.
His record of 581 points in a season
was only bettered in 1982. Tragically
he died of cancer at the age of thirty-
three. He was remembered each year
when the outstanding sportsman was
awarded the Sam Doble trophy. This is
the cover of his testimonial programme.

Mrs Meacham's form group at Northfield School, *c. 1978. Back row, left to right*: Tony Hunter, Kurt Warwood, -?- , Chris ?, Gary Maybury. *Third row*: -?-, James Bott, -?-, Derek Harrigan, Gary Whitehouse, -?-, Darren ?. *Second row*: Mark Mills, Sarah Duffy, Teresa Oakley, Dawn Cooper, Christine White, Michelle Hunt, Debbie Westwood, -?-, -?-. *Front row*: Susan Robins, -?-, Michelle Morris, Marie Langford, Mrs Meacham, Trudy Little, Penny Rose, Ann Banks, Marie Parkinson.

Laurie Green (seated), headmaster of Northfield School, is pictured at his retirement presentation, July 1978. John Light, who is standing in front of him, became acting headmaster, and later Chris James became head. Teacher of English Richard Harding is in the background.

Road safety lessons conducted by local police officers at Trescott Junior School, 1979.

Pupils show off the school uniform at Trescott, *c.* 1979.

7

The 1980s

Pupils from Northfield School celebrate the fiftieth anniversary of the school in 1983 in spectacular style.

Bellfield School is in the centre of this aerial view, summer 1981. The block at the bottom is the Grosvenor Shopping Centre and across the road by the bus is the Bell pub. Behind it, and running left to right is Ulwine Drive; Vineyard Road leads off it and goes to the top right-hand corner. The open space to the left is the Merritt's Brook playing fields and allotments.

The Davenports pub, the Bell, was demolished in 1983, the date of this photograph. It was replaced by a much smaller pub, an architectural monstrosity, which has since been converted into shops, but alas the architectural style remains!

The Trescott Schools celebrated their Golden Jubilee in June 1981. The junior age pupils held a glittering re-enactment of a traditional May Festival. The Lord Mayor of Birmingham, Cllr Ken Barton, attended to crown the Jubilee Queen, Tina Ward, aged eleven.

Jubilee Queen Tina Ward was attended by Emma Hope, Tracey Everitt, Mandy Miller, Karen Corbally, Sarah Spotswood, Samantha Lee, Tracey McDonald, Andrina Thomas, Sarah Fellows, Juliette Reid and page boy Carl Spotswood. Trescott School cook Mrs Howard baked a special Jubilee cake, which as you'd expect had fifty candles on it!

End of term for the top classes, taught by Pat Everest and Neil Spalding, at Trescott in 1983. Sharon Mellon took this photograph of her schoolmates as they prepared to leave Trescott for the final time before going to secondary school. *Back row, left to right*: Lisa Bench, Rosemary Farquarson, Anita Haines, Kim Lane, Lisa Bourne, Cherie Deakin, Christian Oliver, Hayley Bishop, -?-, Darren Clement, Dean Hardware, Alan Breeze, -?-, Kenneth Marshall, Joanne Breeze, Michelle Whiston, Louise Yates. *Second row*: Michelle Hughes, Gillian Shale, Jean Reilly, Angela Riordan, Dean Favell, Peter Williams, -?-, Sarah Reid, Julian Poole, -?-, Perry Malpass, Jane Deeley, Simon Burke. Kneeling at the front are Anthony Johnston, Nicholas Hill, Ursula Ivory, Elizabeth McMurdie, Michael ?, -?-, David Biggs.

Bob Carter at the piano with a group at Trescott, *c.* 1980. Mr Carter was also a session pianist at the BBC.

Northfield Youth Club's annual raft race, June 1985. The teams set off from Arley and paddled along the River Severn, hoping to finish at Bewdley Yacht Club. Pictured are Doreen Wilkes, Lee Howard, Alison Mogford and Gary Wilkes.

Above: In November 1981 a group of pupils from Ley Hill took part in a 'living history' project as part of a visit to Bell Heath study centre. Pupils made uniforms from old blankets, chain mail from ring pulls from cans and re-enacted life in thirteenth- and fourteenth-century Britain. The 'medieval army' stormed Goodrich Castle near Ross-on-Wye.

Right: In January 1986 Glenys Kinnock visited the newly commissioned Nursery Unit at Ley Hill. She unveiled a plaque and class 5C 'presented her with a basket of home made peppermint creams'. With her is headteacher Mr Ratcliffe and John Spellar, the Labour parliamentary candidate. She later visited BBC Pebble Mill to celebrate the thirty-fifth anniversary of the radio programme *The Archers*.

Far right: The brochure produced for the opening of the Nursery Unit. Among other things the unit aimed to 'provide stimulation to motivate children in the development of personal, social, physical, emotional and educational skills'.

'Modern technology' reaches Northfield School! Colin Shuck and Dean Hoban operate one of the first computers used by pupils, in 1982.

A second-year English class at Northfield School, 1981, which took place in the new block added adjacent to the geography and commerce block. The pupils taking advantage of this small group teaching method are Paul Biggs, Dawn White, Dean Genders and Chris Wood.

Northfield School's harvest festival, October 1982. Over seventy parcels were sent to local people and the school band played at a service at St Bartholomew's Church. Teacher John Malpass designed the mural. Such activities were associated with veteran teacher Cath Curtis. Miss Curtis, who taught at Tinker's Farm/Northfield School for twenty-four years retired in 1980, but often came back to help Mr Malpass and Mr Broomfield with their administrative duties. On her retirement she told *Gallery*, the school's newspaper, that it was Miss Walmesley's belief that a monk named Allen, first put his preaching cross as early as AD 670 at Allen's Cross where St Bartholomew's Church now stands. 'Our fifty years is a very small pebble in the pool of this great time, but its ripples have travelled far. For the great blessing of Northfield has always been the quality of certain of the people, staff, parents and children, which it has brought together over this time. Their warmth is hard to find elsewhere. They did not turn their sail to every wind that blowed. They sought excellence in whatever material came in hand. They made every effort worthwhile. May the constancy of their friendship, continue to sustain us, though time and distance may divide. In the words of Matthew Arnold's beautiful poem, written in dark days, "Let us be true to one another".'

In March 1984 The Queen's Own Hussars visited Northfield School on a recruitment drive. They gave a careers talk and drove their Scorpion armoured cars around the playground. David Parker and Chris Bourne are among the pupils in the forward assault of the two Scorpions on show. The school logbook records: 'The sight of these driving around the Kelby Close playground is something many pupils will remember for a long time.'

The staff of Northfield School in November 1982. *Back row, left to right*: Roger Sturman, Dave Colvin, Sean Wilson, Stuart Turner, Bob Hill, Frank Charlton. *Third row*: Graham Slater, Broj Barua, Don Hazzard, Richard Sanders, Clive Murch, Richard Harding, Bob Kendall, Phil ?, temporary caretaker, Angus MacDonald, Margaret Alcock, Jayne Newton, Pauline Quayle. *Second row*: Lawrence Inman, supply teacher, Margaret Smith, Sue Plimley, Ian Nelson, Martin Berry, Steve Packer, Jayne Paterson, Betty Duggan, secretary, Norman Bartlam, Chris Field, Ann Meacheam, Douglas Fleming. *Front row*: Roy Smith, Maureen McGrath, caretaker's wife, Viv Hind, Mandy Ward, John Meyrick, Kay Spiller, Michael Evanson, headmaster, Chris James, John Malpass, Barbara Healey, lab technician, Helen Howard, Dorothy Livesley, secretary, Jennifer Clark.

Tree-mendous news for Northfield School. All of these pupils were prizewinners in the annual Tree Lover's League competition, April 1983. Behind them stand the two large oak trees that were to survive the demolition of the school: the new estate was built around them.

Each year the Northfield School minibus was decorated to make it look as if Santa's sleigh was on top of it. The Northfield School PTA together with a number of teachers and pupils then collected for charity as the float, playing Christmas music, toured the streets at night raising money for good causes. On other occasions teachers and PTA members dressed in medieval costumes as 'Knights of Mirth' and toured pubs collecting as they went. Sadly, no photos seem to exist of this. Shame!

The pupils who collected money on the Northfield School Christmas float. This was the group in 1982 or 1983 with Santa Bartlam. This photo was developed by a pupil in Mr Nelson's photography group.

Northfield School appeared on the BBC TV programme *We Are The Champions*. The team finished third in the final after becoming English champions, scoring a record number of points in the heats. Pictured are Warren Little, Alan Mills, Simon Jewell, Adrian Woodward, Mandy Miller, Jackie Carter, Tracey Robbins and Madeline Meier.

Supporters from Northfield School watch a recording of *We Are the Champions*. The programme was a cross between a junior version of *Superstars* and *It's A Knock Out*. Ron Pickering presented the programme with the help of athletes Gary and Heather Oakes and Tessa Sanderson.

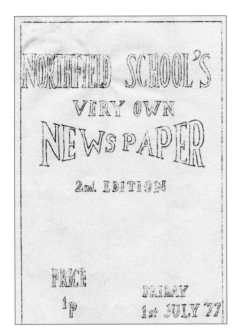

Above, left: In 1977 Northfield School produced its own newspaper under the guidance of Miss Spiller. It was called *Gallery*. The newspaper developed over the years with the help of the author of this book, Norman Bartlam, and kept going until the school closed in 1986. *Right:* The June 1982 edition of *Gallery* contained a preview of the World Cup and a wall chart. This edition also featured the camping trip to Snowdonia with Mr Nelson and Mr Sanders, and the cricket victory over Bournville, with Dave Parker and Andy Palmer top scoring.

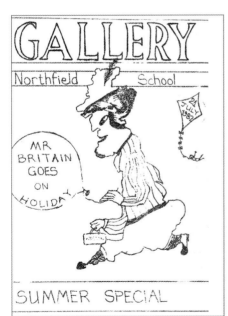

Above, left: The July 1982 edition featured summer holiday activities as well as stories about the Duke of Edinburgh Awards, a visit to BBC Pebble Mill, and a goodbye to Mrs Stott, who had been head of English for six years. *Right:* Technology improved and the school bought a photocopier which could copy photographs! The March 1984 edition featured a photograph on the cover for the first time. It showed the basketball team that won the South Birmingham Schools Basketball League, winning all ten of the matches played.

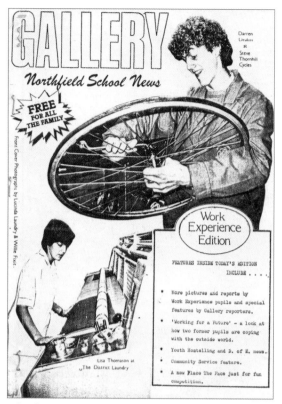

The Christmas 1982 edition of *Gallery*, which featured the Duke of Edinburgh Award winners, the retirement of Mr Zielinski after twenty years of service to Northfield and Tinker's Farm, the school band which played in the Bull Ring and a look at Christmas events in past years.

The front cover of a Work Experience edition of *Gallery* featuring Darren Deakin and Lisa Thomason. The work experience programme at the school was recognised as one of the best in the city. The programme, which saw pupils undertake work-based placements, was organised by Bob Hill and Angie Marshall.

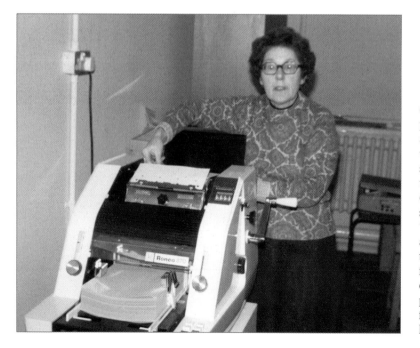

Gallery's state of the art presses are galvanised into action by Dot Liveseley, who, along with fellow secretary Betty Duggan, typed and duplicated *Gallery*. An entry in the school logbook reads: '*Gallery* continues to report all that is happening and to be a good advertisement for this school.' Special *Gallery* joke books were produced to help raise funds to subsidise youth-hostelling trips.

The girls of Northfield School won the King's Norton & District Netball League in 1983. They included Dawn Selman, Mandy Burkett and Teresa Flynn. The school logbook records: 'as the numbers in the school decline our sporting achievements have declined. This year however the netball teams have been extremely successful. Mrs Hind is to be congratulated on her efforts.' Two years earlier girls from the school won the trampoline championships under the direction of Miss Harris. The girls were Theresa Oakley, Marie Parkinson, Debbie Westwood and Charlotte Donnelley.

Northfield School geographers at work, October 1985. Richard Jeffries and Arshead Hussein test their geography skills.

Northfield School followed the Tinker's Farm tradition of producing quality drama. In 1984 the school play was watched by one of the largest audiences ever seen for such a production. The school logbook records: 'Johnny Salter was a huge success. I was especially pleased at the support which came from the inspectorate and all those who came said how they had enjoyed it, making helpful constructive comments. Many members of staff were involved and upwards of 50 pupils in one way or another. Mr Slater and Mr Bradney were the producers and the whole event demonstrated just what can be achieved in this sphere in Northfield.' The wartime play *Run Rabbit Run* was directed by G. Slater and Richard Harding.

A group of hostellers at Ffestiniog, April 1983. *Gallery* reported: 'Ffourth and ffifth year pupils went to ffantastic Ffestiniog in Norff Wales, the hostel has ffabulous ffacilities and is surrounded by ffootpaths, ffences, ffresh fflowers and ffertile ffields. It was ffrequented by ffriendly ffolk ffrom Norffield.' The teachers are Chris Evans, on the right, and Stuart Turner at the back. Hostel warden Sue Tugwell is also in the photograph.

A youth hostelling trip to Stow-on-the-Wold, *c*. 1982. The three teachers on the right of the bridge are Chris Field, Richard Sanders and Dougie Fleming. The seated pupil is Nicholas Robotham. In 1983 staff gave up their own time to take pupils on no fewer than thirteen weekend hostelling, Duke of Edinburgh Award and day trips. In June alone there were two hostelling trips to Dolgellau, day visits to Dovedale and Chatterley Whitfield Mining Museum, and residential weekends at Windmill House and Ogwen Cottage Outdoor Pursuits Centre.

A youth hostelling trip to Ludlow, September 1982. The pupils are Sarah Dyer, Tracey Robbins, Tracey MacDonald, Lisa Thomason, Stuart ?, Jason Hyde (who is partly hidden), Chris Brady, Darren Deakin and Jeffrey ?. The teachers on this visit were Messrs Fleming, Wilson, Bartlam and Miss Plimley. Ludlow was always a popular place for Northfield School's weekend hostelling trips. Demand often outstripped supply and Mr Nelson used his own minibus so that more pupils could go on the trips. In March 1982 Diane Richards wrote in *Gallery*: 'we went on a night walk which ended at the castle which was supposed to be haunted. We had a walk which was about 5,000 million miles long.' She was told a million times not to exaggerate!

Youth hostelling to a farm in Stow, *c.* 1982.

Youth hostelling reaches new depths in September 1982. A group of pupils, led by teacher Kay Spiller, prepare to descend to the bottom of the Llechwedd Slate Caverns near Ffestiniog.

Breakfast time at Ludlow youth hostel, May 1983. Making a meal of things are Vanda Bradley, Emma Hope, Caroline Biggs and Lisa Thomson.

Northfield School's final youth-hostelling trip was a week-long visit for twenty-eight pupils to Exeter in June 1985. The teachers who organised the trip were Stuart Turner, Viv Hind, Keith Tromans and Norman Bartlam. The photograph shows most of the group. *Back row*: Norman Bartlam, Chris Bourne, Lee Deadman, Ian Matthews, Paul Hartigan, Peter Cross, Wayne McMullan. *Second row*: Ian and Sue Tugwell, the wardens, Kerry Mountjoy, Dawn Selman, Sharon Dexter, -?-, Viv. Hind, -?-, Julie Lacey, Trudi Featherstone, Jayne Wood, Alison Mogford, Vince ?, assistant warden. *Front row*: Jon Cooper, Alan Emmison, Thomas Pickering, -?-, -?-, Kevin Bradley, Dean Hoban, Robert Sands, Gary Parker, -?-, Margaret ?, hostel warden. In the same term Mr Hazzard, Miss Plimley and Mrs Smith took seventeen pupils to Ilam Hall in Derbyshire. The school logbook records: 'Both courses were excellent and showed a great deal of commitment from the staff concerned.'

Northfield School developed a highly regarded Duke of Edinburgh Awards scheme. Here Pamela Brady takes part in an exercise with a fire hydrant at Northfield Fire Station in November 1981.

Northfield School's work experience programme and Personal Achievement Record Scheme were the envy of many other schools.

The fiftieth anniversary celebrations at Northfield School. It was a freezing cold day in February 1983 when this photograph was taken to publicise the celebrations. In order to do this the school 'borrowed' a fire engine with a hydraulic platform from Northfield Fire Station. Teacher John Meyrick and photographers from the *Northfield Messenger* and *Birmingham Evening Mail* snapped away! The result was this very effective photograph, which appeared in both newspapers more than once.

The hydraulic platform is moved into position in the playground as pupils begin lining up in the shape of a fifty. Kelby Close is in the background.

As part of the fiftieth anniversary celebrations the team behind the school newspaper appealed through the local press for photographs and memorabilia. This publicity photograph appeared in the *Evening Mail* in November 1982. Pictured is Norman Bartlam (second left), co-editor of the school newspaper *Gallery*; and a geography teacher at the school. With him are some of the newspaper's reporting team: Colin Burbridge, Pamela Brady, Karen Price, Lisa Moody and Dena Ryall. Heather Soady is seated at the desk next to their young-looking teacher!

A competition was held to see how far around the world the news about the school's fiftieth anniversary could get. This is Valerie Eccles, née Bennett, who was May Queen in 1951 (see page 83). She wrote from her home in Canada to say: 'I am sure that like myself you feel very proud to be part of a fine school. Many things have changed since I was at Tinker's Farm. I was sad to hear that the May Festival is no more, but things move on and change and one must remember with great happiness those wonderful days in May when work was put aside and we had a wonderful time in crowning our new head girl. A wonderful spirit prevailed in the school, there were spring flowers everywhere and different forms performed plays and entertainment. We were very proud indeed. I wish you good luck in your future endeavours and send fond greetings from Toronto to the school which I shall always hold close to my heart.'

A. Ingram wrote from Johannesburg to recall his days at Tinker's Farm Boys' School in the 1960s.

Three members of staff at Northfield School at the time of the fiftieth anniversary celebrations were former pupils at the Tinker's Farm Girls' School. Head of upper school John Meyrick has a word to say to lab technician Barbara Healey, secretary Betty Duggan and cleaner Joan Marshall.

Northfield School's fiftieth anniversary celebrations included a very effective exhibition of Tinker's Farm at war, devised by history teacher Doug Fleming. Pupils include Mandy O'Meara, Lee Taylor and Teresa Flynn.

'As I approached the school gates from Kelby Close I gazed in awe at the playground of my younger days that I had not trodden on since I left school in 1935. It was a great pleasure to meet three of your staff, the secretary who was most kind and helpful, your keen, active and enthusiastic Mr Bartlam and Mrs Barbara Healey a friend of all my family years ago. I returned to the exhibition with my granddaughter'.

William Holland

'It was a wonderful trip down memory lane. I think I most enjoyed looking at the old photographs and I admired the way you had presented them'.

Doreen Rice

'May I take this opportunity to convey my heartfelt thanks for making last Friday evening the most enjoyable of my life. I can't express enough now marvellous it was meeting up with so many old school friends whom I hadn't seen for over thirty years. I must congratulate you on how expertly everything had been put together'.

Josephine Boorn, née Laight

Cllr Bill Sowton, who was Lord Mayor elect, and Cllr Mrs Florrie Pickering JP who was chairman of the school governors, officially opened the fiftieth anniversary celebrations which consisted of a whole weekend of displays and activities. Headmaster Mike Evanson is in the centre of the photograph. Early visitors to the exhibition included Miss Aslin, Northfield MP John Spellar, and a distinguished former pupil, Doris Satchwell, now Baroness Doris Fisher of Rednal.

Head of geography Don Hazzard with geography teacher Norman Bartlam at a display about the changing face of Northfield. The school's temporary caretaker is in the centre, making sure that not too much mess is made on the floor!

Getting the message across . . . (from left) Karen Skelding, Sharon Dexter, Diane Richards and Julie Lacey outside Northfield school.

July 1982

Save Our School

Our school, Northfield, is one of the best in the district and we don't want it to close. Some people have the wrong impression of our school. There are many activities and it also acts as a youth club, which many people use.

We have raised a large sum of money to buy a guide dog for the blind. We do get positive results from this school because we have experienced teachers and hardworking pupils. We want our school to stay open for our benefit and for future generations.

Our school is quite small — but the smaller the better. Each pupil gets individual attention. Those needing help get it. When the Conservatives came to power all Labour plans were withdrawn and we would like to know what is going on! Children's education, what is going to suffer and parents' pockets too, in bus fares.

Northfield is not just another school, it is OUR school and we want it to stay open.

Julie Lacey,
Karen Skelding,
Sharon Dexter,
Northfield School,
Northfield.

In the early 1980s a reorgansation of schools took place. This spelt the end for some small, supposedly uneconomic schools, including Northfield. The decision to close Northfield School was made in 1982. Staff, pupils and governors fought to keep the school open. Mrs Florrie Pickering, chairman of Northfield School Governors, handed in a petition signed by over 1,000 people. She praised the school and its role in the life of the Allen's Cross area. Pupils Karen Skelding, Sharon Dexter, Diane Richards and Julie Lacey took their protest to the local press stating: 'Our school is quite small – but the smaller the better. Each pupil gets individual attention. Those needing help get it. Northfield School is not just another school it is OUR school.'

1986 nf lastweek0001.JPG

Northfield School's last ten — left to right, Jason Butt, Paul Oakley, Mark Brittle, Mark Brant, Hazel Joy, Elizabeth McMurdie, Rachel Bailey, Michael Smith, Richard Jeffries and Arshead Hussain

School's out...

There was, sadly, a long lingering death, with Northfield School's intake and staff gradually reduced. Eventually the two outer buildings, the former junior and infant schools were closed and the science labs, opened at considerable expense less than ten years earlier, were also closed. Mrs Schneider was drafted in to see through the closure. The last day of secondary education was Friday 18 July 1986. The last ten pupils were pictured in the *Evening Mail*. *Left to right*: Jason Butt, Paul Oakley, Mark Brittle, Mark Brant, Hazel Joy, Elizabeth McMurdie, Rachel Bailey, Michael Smith, Richard Jeffries and Arshead Hussain. A thanksgiving service for Tinker's Farm/Northfield School, and of all pupils and staff was held at St Bartholomew's Church on 16 July 1986, and another service was held on Sunday 12 April 1987 for the dedication of the Paschal Candle stand.

Ley Hill staff, *c.* 1988. *Standing, left to right*: Kay Bayliss, Jo James, Eleanor Wright, Judy Thompson, Rhoda Rowlands, Carol McGowan, Tracey Cameron, Amanda Spencer, Sheila Swan, Di Johns. *Seated*: Helen Windsor, Stuart Turner, Alan Ratcliffe, Margaret Ward, Rob Tredwell.

8

Recent Years

June 2000, demolition of the hall at Tinker's Farm Northfield school.

Ley Hill School celebrated its fortieth anniversary in autumn 1994. A Jubilee-style street party was held in the playground. The houses in the background are on Rhayader Road. The Lord Mayor, Cllr R. Knowles, attended the anniversary assembly, which included the memories of Mr Arnold, headmistress 1968–78. Pupils performed events of the 1950s, including 'Watch With Mother'!

Dramatic changes have taken place in the area around Ulwine Drive. There were two reasons for this. Firstly the quality of the maisonettes was poor and it was cheaper to demolish and rebuild rather than repair them, and secondly work began to clear the land for the Northfield bypass, something that was first planned in 1948!

The end of Vineyard Road as we knew it! The last maisonette is demolished to make way for a new housing estate.

As an exercise in active citizenship pupils from Bellfield Infants' School took part in a project to help design the new play area, which was built on the new estate. They were given a fixed budget and area of land to work on. The selected designs were put up before a judging panel and voted for in a democratic ballot, which was overseen by local councillors Sir Richard Knowles and the long serving Ray Holtom.

The Bellfield Regeneration project was set up by the author of this book as part of his work with the Housing Education Initiative. The project won a major award from the Institute of Housing for the way the council involved young people in regeneration issues. Here Norman Bartlam is with some of the pupils who worked on the project.

That's the spirit! Local resident Betty Howard checks the walls are level on the first new house on Vineyard Road, assisted by pupils from Bellfield School.

Bellfield Infant School pupils pose with Dennis Minnis, the chairman of the city's housing committee, when he visited the area to see the progress being made on the new estate.

While the work was continuing at Merritt's Brook the Tinker's Farm site was being emptied ready for demolition. This May 2000 view shows the rear of the caretaker's house looking towards Tinker's Farm Road from the library corridor of Northfield School.

The two large oak trees which dominated the skyline in the Merritt's Brook playing fields survived the upheaval and are now on the side of the new road. The new £15 million development contains 230 homes.

The Lord Mayor of Birmingham arrives to visit Mrs Crockett, the oldest person living in the new Bellfield estate development. Her home is a bungalow on Vineyard Road.

Northfield School as it looked from the Tinker's Farm Road side, May 1982. The newer block of four classrooms on the left, although planned to ease the overcrowding bought on by the raising of the school leaving age in 1971 to sixteen, were not completed until 1977. The lower rooms were use for mathematics and the upper ones for small group lessons in basic subjects, see page 132. Behind it were similar blocks built for geography and commerce.

Above, left: Sharing happy memories as the school crumbles are Barbara and Ken Healey. Ken was a pupil at Tinker's Farm Boys' School and he met his wife Barbara Allen at the school in the 1940s. Barbara later worked there, see page 146. *Right:* Another couple in the same spot as Ken and Barbara, but this time sixty years earlier. Mr and Mrs Taylor, the school caretakers, stand with the tallest part of the school visible in the background. The hut behind them on the left is part of the original building at the school.

A poignant end to Tinker's Farm/Northfield School, 6 June 2000. The broken sign is outside the now demolished caretaker's house, revealing the shattered façade of a once proud building.

Twisted steel girders from the former Northfield School Upper School, formerly Tinker's Farm Junior School, frame the façade of the main building on the Kelby Close side of the school.

The Tinker's Farm Road, side of Northfield School, May 2000. It was always rumoured that time capsules had been created in glass bottles, which were put in place by workmen when the building was erected. Two bottles were said to have been placed in the centre of the stone circles above the top windows on both sides of the building. There was great excitement and ultimately even greater disappointment when the stone circles proved to be only decorative features! The centre of the stones was filled with glass bottles but these were broken off, and so were only a few inches long: three were empty and one stuffed only with the wrapper used on the roof felt!

This was once a pathway along which many thousands of children entered the school from Tinker's Farm Road. Now the sound of pounding feet and children's chatter is replaced by silence, a silence soon to be replaced by the drone of bulldozers as they destroyed the fabric, but not the memories, of a once grand building.

Demolition of the Tinker's Farm side of the Northfield School building, June 2000.

Smashed and destroyed. The Kelby Close side of the building seen from behind shattered glass in the former Infant School building, which in later years became the City Council's Neighbourhood Office.

In June 2000 a well-attended exhibition was held at Northfield Library to commemorate the history of the schools. A number of former pupils and teachers met up to discuss the 'good old days'. Pictured left to right are a number of pupils who attended Northfield School in the early to mid-1980s: Jackie Carter, Andrew Steenton, David Bishop, Simon Jewell and Alan Mills. With them is former geography teacher and author of this book Norman Bartlam who organised the exhibition. Most of the pupils are on page 136.

The Housing Education Initiative involved local people and Trescott pupils in a local history project to suggest the name for the new roads to be built on the Tinker's Farm site. School council members spoke about the project on BBC Radio WM. This photograph shows Carl Chinn of BBC WM with Sharon Mellon, Robert Sands and Elizabeth Parker.

The new estate takes shape on the site of Northfield School in February 2001. The two tall oak trees managed to survive the demolition. They can be seen on the photograph on pages 14 and 32. The path leads into the new toddlers' playground.

One of the new streets is called Walmesley Way after the foundation headmistress of the Tinker's Farm schools.

The landscape is changing still further. The blocks of flats at Ley Hill have been demolished and will soon be replaced by a new housing estate. Meanwhile, the work of Ley Hill School and Trescott continues.

Richard Burden, Labour MP for Northfield, was joined in June 2002 by two pupils who were looking to the future as he planted a tree to celebrate Trescott's seventieth birthday.

Acknowledgements

Thanks to everyone who contacted me with photographs or information for this book. Even with 160 pages (the standard book in this series runs to 128 pages) there was not enough room to fit every one's photographs in. Particular thanks to the following people and organisations. Bellfield School: Gayle Flynn, Marion Sedgewick. Trescott School: Jackie Gazeley and Jenny Whitehouse, Mrs Bennett, Sharon Mellon, Ron Harrison, Dorothy Bilbrough. Ley Hill School: Stuart Turner and the staff. Northfield Library: Lesley Sedgewick and Sue Teckoe. Ex-Northfield School staff: Don Hazzard, Sue Hazzard, John Meyrick, Stuart Turner. Ex-Tinker's Farm and Northfield pupils: John Bennett, Ivan Parker, Sylvia Owen, née James, Betty Smith, Barbara Healey, née Allen, Ken Healey, Doris Tack, Dawn Taylor, née Stewartson, Grace Sewell, née McGann, Brenda Daniels, née Gould, Josie Cardwell, Marie Langford. Other individuals: Betty Howard, Eileen Doyle, Tony Spettigue, Richard Albutt, Mrs B. Hyett, *Birmingham Evening Mail*, *Northfield Messenger* and anyone else who contacted me with messages via the Friends Reunited website.